Overcome Dumpster Juice Beliefs to Become Excellent in All You Do!

EZELL L. BARNES
- AKA -
"Chef Zoagie"
Foreword by Saquion Gullett

Copyright © 2024 by Ezell Barnes
All rights reserved.

No part of this publication may be reproduced, distributed, or transmitted in any form or by any means, including photocopying, recording, or other electronic or mechanical methods, without the prior written permission of the publisher, except in the case of brief quotations embodied in critical reviews and certain other noncommercial uses permitted by copyright law.

For permission requests, write to the publisher, addressed "Attention: Permissions Coordinator," at the address below.
Ingramspark.com

Ordering Information:
Quantity sales. Special discounts are available on quantity purchases by corporations, associations, and others. For details, contact the author at the address above.

Printed in the United States of America

ISBN 979-8-8693-8150-7

Dedication

This book was started seven years ago and I have been POOP JUICE with getting it published. It is finally here, and I want to dedicate this to me, EZELL BARNES. I also want to dedicate this book to all my family and friends who had to hear me talk about it and have been patiently waiting for its birth. Lastly, I dedicate this to my Pop, who is no longer here to see that his son became his favorite saying, "A man made of muscle, knock a train off its tussle, and make a bulldog hustle."

Table of Contents

Foreword — vii

Introduction — ix

You Can Change In A Moment! — 3

Excellent PrinciplesAnd Beliefs — 10

Size Does Matter — 13

90 Days Of Extreme Effort = Excellence — 26

You Have To See It And Believe It — 31

Another Moment In Time — 35

Sports Revisited — 40

You Must Speak, Believe, Work, Then Achieve — 44

Keep Those That Believe In You Around! — 52

Same Recipe For Super Athletic Gains — 55

Business Excellence! — 58

Only Take Advice From The Best!	64
Write Out Your Life And Relationship Goals!	71
Go From Fat To Fit, Just Be Consistent!	89
Million-Dollar Idea	94
Divine Universal Favor	100
Official From Back Yard To Uptown	104
Out Of Town, Love Social Media Reach	109
Opportunity	115
Be Zifferent	118
You Are A Prophet	124
Relentless Pursuit	137
Burning Desire	142
Overcome Obstacles/Hate	147
Stay Focused On The End	156
Every Idea Doesn't Work	160
Influence	163
Keep Searching	173
Nothing Is Guaranteed	176
A True Hustler	181
You Win Or You Learn	184

Applied Knowledge Is Wisdom	186
Stay Creative	188
Pandemic Proof	191
Always Reach Up	194
There Is More Than One Way	197
Do More, Become More	202
More Money, More Problems	205
Fighting For The $1,000,000 Finish	210
New Beginnings, New Goals	214
One Last Story And Advice	216

Foreword

The practice of alchemy is most often attributed to medieval times, but its earliest origins can be found in text dating back to nearly 100 BC. Part chemistry and part magic, it was believed that anyone who perfected this craft would be able to most notably change lead into gold. Modern-day alchemists like Ezell Barnes don't spend their days actually looking to change the matter of metals.

Instead, they take life's ordinary situations and turn them into something extraordinary in ways that, until now, most thought were unexplainable. Ezell or "Zoke", as he is called by those like myself who know him best, has taken on this alchemy on two separate levels.

Not only has he mastered the art of bending the world around him and altering reality to meet his life's goals, but he has also taken on the task of molding that magical process into steps that you also can follow to become a modern-day alchemist in your own right. It took years. The process didn't happen overnight, but he sifted out all of the impurities and is now ready to hand you a shiny piece of proverbial gold.

In my estimation, Eazy Excellence doesn't necessarily mean that excellence is easy, but it does show you that it is a lot more attainable than you may think. Just put in the work and use the power of your mind to create an unstoppable force. I've personally watched Zoke go on a mental journey to find the universal elixir and manifest it in many ways from increased physical ability to finances and even weight loss. I've been at him for years about putting this book out because I believe that it will help people. I knew that he had found a way for people to unlock potential that they probably didn't know they had.

I am honored to have a small part in this project because I've had a front-row seat to the excellence that he is about to tap into. I'm sublimely excited about that.

I will be waiting anxiously for a new wave of extraordinary people. A fresh group who will, in time, learn to operate without limitations. There's a quote that says, "Things are impossible until they're not," and Zoke will take you to a place where the only words in that quote that are real to you are the last two. Nothing is impossible here. It is how he lives, it is how he breathes. It is how he talks, it is how he sees. He walks under the strong belief that whatever you want, you can have. The painstaking process of alchemy has been done, and he is handing you his universal elixir. Ingest and enjoy…

INTRODUCTION

Have you ever found yourself not performing at the level you want in different areas of your life? Ever wanted to be great but not able to get past your current level?

All people want to be good at whatever they are involved in, but most are average or below-average performers. I call them POOP JUICE performers because it is directly linked to dumpster juice beliefs. They are more commonly known as negative beliefs and, unfortunately, they are far too common. These belief systems should be disposed of and avoided at all costs because they stink and spread to everyone who entertains them. In order to make a mark in the world we live in today, you MUST be well above average. You should aim to be EXCELLENT because anything else is normal. Normal never achieves, it just survives.

Very few people become excellent at what they do, but excellence can be achieved the EZ way by anyone doing anything! In this book, I will share some of my sport, business, health, spiritual, and relationship stories about how I overcame being POOP JUICE and became excellent at just about everything. Throughout the book, you will see how different my life became when I applied the principles and methods of excellence compared to the times when I did not. You will learn how to become who you want to be, how to believe in yourself when no one else does, what causes you to transform practically overnight and definitely within 90 days, and what it takes to live an excellent life by excelling in all you are involved in.

CHAPTER 1

YOU CAN CHANGE IN A MOMENT!

You know opening this book can change your life forever, right? I know you didn't open it because you know it all or exhibit excellence in all you do. Most likely, you are POOP JUICE somewhere in your business, personal, social, or spiritual life! You're discontented with your situation as it now stands and it is driving you to search for answers and direction to achieve your goals. You want more. I know because I feel it and remember it. You want to be better than you are. You want to be excellent, and excellence starts with a decision made at a moment in time.

If you study the greats, you will see most of their lives are driven by one moment in time when they made a decision. You usually find your back against a wall, where it is do or die, or something in you just drives you to go in the opposite direction of the one you were previously heading. Life-changing decisions happen in a moment!

I grew up in Salem City, New Jersey. Salem is a place where most only pass through, but I love it and still call it home. Salem was and still is a poor, crime-filled place, but at the same time, it has beautiful people from there who should be admired. It was tough growing up in a town where most of the minority homes were broken. I was a lucky one who had an active father, but at times, not so lucky because I think some of my peers felt shorted and took it out on me. Overall, I was cool with most people, but I just tried not to stand out too much to avoid creating enemies. As a kid, sports were a good outlet for us all, but I was not that good at any. I was POOP JUICE.

I got cut from the Mullica Hill Mites pee wee football team because I did not apply myself, and at the same time, I was a little scared of my rough teammates. This was a result of "DUMPSTER JUICE BELIEFS".

I somehow allowed fear to keep me from trying my best and, therefore, was not worthy of making the team. I had the dumpster juice belief that my teammates were better than me. Allowing your mind to harbor fear will always limit your effectiveness and stop whatever you're trying to accomplish. A couple of years later, I tried out and made it on the Oaks Midget League football team. I was a tight end. I was ok at catching and running the ball but nothing spectacular.

I was pretty much a "POOP JUICE PERFORMER". If you were good at football, you got respect in the city, and although I wanted respect, I did not want to step on toes and have to fight. All that changed in a moment!

Later that football season, when I was 13 years old, my team was getting killed by the Bridgeton team. The score was around 30 to nothing and it was cold and dark. Their team seemed too big to be playing us. They felt like a pro team against us kids and were hurting our top players left and right. I remember getting in the game and the next play was a pass to me. I was so nervous that out of the huddle, I split wide to get away from everyone, but my quarterback called me back tight. After I came back, the defensive end stared at me and said with a deep voice, "8-man line." I was frozen with fear, the ball hiked and I tried to block him and missed. From here, he sacked the quarterback, most likely because I forgot to go out for the pass, not to mention I was shaking in my boots. Now, the coach pulled me out of the game and sat me on the bench— I was actually happy to be out of harm's way. There were about five minutes left in the game and my coach had this great idea of putting me back in. Coach asked me a question that would change my life forever, *"Will you run an end around for me?"*

I pondered, looked at the score, and thought to myself, "I may be young but I'm smart. And there is no way I can help and will end up getting hurt." I accepted defeat and told the coach, "NO." Immediately, I felt an overwhelming feeling of regret. It was like time stopped and I just felt like I embarrassed my father and the Barnes family name.

My dad always would tell me as a child that he was "A man made of muscle, knock a train off its tussle, and make a bulldog hustle, how strong are you, son?" I would look up to him with my tiny body and say, "I am stronger than you, Daddy!" Well, at that moment, I was scared and definitely not stronger than my dad. From that moment, I decided I would never be afraid or back down from anything else ever again.

On the bus ride home and all through the night, I visualized myself being a monster on the field. I focused on that image so intensely, that the next day, I was a terror in practice. I really went from passive to a powerful, aggressive, and dominant player overnight. My coaches and teammates were astonished. They were like, "How can he go from being scared to enter a game and overnight trying to hit anything moving?" Wow, what a feeling! Just by allowing the fear to go and fully applying myself!

I immediately catapulted as an athlete, by leaps and bounds overnight. This is proof that fear and dumpster juice beliefs are the #1 culprit in keeping one from obtaining their unlocked potential. By getting rid of the fear of the unknown, you are able to try your best and see where it takes you, which is usually to places unimaginable. Today, you can decide that you will put away the fear. It actually is that simple and a choice you can make at any moment. I am hoping you do before finishing this book.

When faced with obstacles, we all have a fight or flight mechanism to help keep us alive, but it also kicks in when faced with some everyday decisions that lead to success or failure. Whether the obstacle is big or small, use wisdom and choose to fight.

There is a time to choose flight by walking away from something that is not working for you, but what's needed to get you to the next level? By taking swift action, fear will disappear, and what seemed like an obstacle in your path will clear. Trust me, don't ponder or hesitate when the emotion of fear creeps up. The longer you ponder, the more likely you will run away from getting what you desire. The motto that keeps me grounded and focused is what my daddy told me. "I am a man made of muscle, knock a train off its tussle, and make a bulldog hustle!" This holds me strong and keeps me motivated to take on the next thing.

CHAPTER 2

EXCELLENT PRINCIPLES AND BELIEFS

To be a winner, you have to be excellent. You can reshape yourself by using principles my mother taught me growing up. Once I started to believe what she taught me, I started applying it and the results were astonishing. From a child, she would have me read quotes from ancient scriptures. *"I can do all things through the anointing which strengthens me"*, *"All things are possible to him that believes"*, *"You are more than a conqueror"*. To keep me grounded, these proverbs stood strong, *"Speak things that are not as if they are and they soon will be"*, *"You must become a prophet and prophecy your future"*, *"You will reap what you sow"*, *"As a man thinks so is he"*. "Faith without work is dead", "Greater is he that is in me than he that is in the world", and to "fear not" were more principles that motivated me and had me trust in something stronger than myself.

I believed these excellent principles wholeheartedly. These principles and beliefs from the ancient scriptures are used in many of the most popular self-help books of today and yesterday. Find me a Great and I will guarantee they used some form of excellent beliefs and principles to achieve success. They say there is nothing new under the sun, but I believe it is new to the person hearing for the first time.

Thinking back to the football league, the following season, I was excellent because of my change in thinking and hard work. I once again played for the Oaks Midget football team, but this year was totally different. That same play my coach asked me to run the year before became our team's number one go-to play.

We could need 15 yards or more and they would call

red end around, which meant to pass to me, and I would always get the first down! That felt great, but I just didn't make it in the end zone that often. I was always bothered by that because it was left to the running backs.

I was now a leader on that team after being one of the POOP JUICE players the year before. It felt good to excel. Actually, it felt great. I was determined to continue this feeling when I was in my freshman year at Salem High School

CHAPTER 3

SIZE DOES MATTER

The size of your vision and dreams will determine the amount of work, faith, and discipline necessary to make them manifest.

If you see yourself as small or inadequate, that's the way you will perform, and also how you will be seen by others. The way people see you is usually a reflection of the way you see yourself. I know many big men that see themselves as small, and that is the way I look at them too. Even when they try to act tough, it is not believable. If you see your business as small, you will treat it that way and others will also. You will grow depending on how big or small you see yourself.

You will always reap what you sow, is what I always believed.

I believed I would be great, so that spring and summer, knowing I only weighed 90 pounds, I began to lift weights and exercise every day. My friends would see me and laugh like I was wasting my time. I paid those with dumpster juice beliefs no mind. Every day I visualized making the team and making big hits. I even told myself I was 6'4", 295 pounds of power, although my reality was 5'6", 90 pounds. I used my imagination for creation and gained a powerful eight pounds of muscle that would have 295lbs of impact. I made the team!

I was combining excellent principles, speaking things that were not, and they became real. I was sowing hard work that others avoided, and I expected to win, so as a freshman, I reaped. I started at fullback—a position designed for the biggest, toughest, and most agile blocker—but I was only 98lbs. The running backs were 200-plus-lbs, and I blocked for them—picture that. I never left the field. I was the hardest hitter on defense playing cornerback. Although tiny in stature, my vision of myself was huge and it impacted everyone around me. Again, my belief was that I worked harder than anyone else, therefore, I felt entitled and was supposed to win... and win I did. I won the hearts of my teammates and put fear in opposing teams. We finished the season 8-1.

I can do anything I believe and it showed. Whenever a person believes with everything in them that they can, they will never be denied. The power of your belief will override your circumstances.

In my sophomore year, I decided to leave the high school and play for a new 130lbs team named The Raiders. I only weighed 110lbs that year. My decision was not a popular one—I was mocked by the upperclassmen and told that I was scared to play varsity that year, which did not make sense because all I did was crush. I used them as motivation.

You will always have POOP JUICE PERFORMERS telling you negative things when you are moving in a new direction. They don't want you to excel too far past them or do things differently from them.

The coach saw differently. He pulled us together and spoke with us to have the intention of winning a championship. We all believed we would. With POOP JUICE performers at my neck, refusing to fail in my spirit, and the vision to win in my mind, I put everything I had into it. I did it with conviction.

Now, let me tell you, there is nothing like being unified and having like-minded people on your team. When you are growing, know this—you should always stay in the company of like-minded people.

Now, this season was crazy because I, unfortunately, broke my wrist in a hard-hitting game. To top that, I was laughed at because it was not in the varsity game. Well, I wrapped my wrist up, never missed a practice, worked very hard, got healthy, and helped my team win the championship.

What was really awesome was to get to the championship, we had to beat Bridgeton, the team that put fear in my heart and embarrassed me a couple of years before. For me, all I was thinking about was payback. I got the chance to crush the guy who put fear in me three years earlier, what a feeling! I scored and had over 10 tackles! This was sweet revenge! The varsity team that year was POOP JUICE, only a .500 team!

Again, you reap what you sow. When you work hard, you should expect to win.

When you believe with your heart, it impacts everyone around you. The following year, I made the varsity team and had to prove myself all over again, and I did. I first smashed the loud mouths that mocked me and then won a starting corner position and backup running back roll. At the huge weight of 125lbs, I was the hardest hitter on the team and helped the team win its first championship in many years. I got my first start at running back in the championship game. I rushed for 135 yards and a touchdown! I became an all-star, and again, a champion in my first-year varsity. I was excellent because of extreme effort, focus, and beliefs that also carried over to the team. The funny thing is, when you conquer your fears and press forward, others will follow and appreciate you for leading the way to excellence.

We won another championship in my senior year! I never left the field and was known as the "Mouth of South Jersey" because not only did I tell myself my goals, I also told my opponents. I knew there was power behind words, especially when you wholeheartedly believe what you are saying. I heard many things about not allowing others to know your goals but I felt the complete opposite. What is for me is for me. I believe once I have spoken a goal in front of others, I now have more fuel to hold myself accountable. Surely, I also knew that the lazy POOP JUICE people would definitely let me know if I did not do what I said, and I refused to be a tool for their laughter. I advise this type of goal setting because it is easier to give up on things when you're the only one holding yourself accountable. Speaking positively or negatively with conviction will always influence others. I would speak with passion to my teammates and they would believe we were unstoppable. We finished the regular season undefeated.

Before games, I would yell to the other team that I was 6'4" 295 pounds, and when they saw my small frame, they would laugh. The first person I saw laugh, I would mark for collision on kick-off. Once the game started, they all believed me after feeling that 295-pound force coming from a 130-pound running back and Safety. I used my words to motivate myself and the team and to frustrate our opponents. At the end of the year, I received honors. I was selected as a first-team All Salem County, Tri-County, and South Jersey Safety at only 130 pounds. Of the graduating class of 1994, the one-time POOP JUICE performer was the only person to be a first-team all-star in three different sports. I am so proud that I am smiling as I write.

Yes, I received all-star honors, not only in football, but in everything I participated in.

I excelled in football, wrestling, and track. I started wrestling when I was just eight years old. I loved the sport because I was fully responsible for my results. I wrestled for the Jr. Rams for three years before they cut our program. I was good but not excellent. By the time I got to high school, I was out of the sport for four years. Only three of my teammates in high school had Jr. Ram experience. Our team as a whole was POOP JUICE. I was a captain on the team and had to wrestle our all-star 171-pounder and heavyweight because of the lack of experience the lighter guys had. It really helped me. I wrestled at 112 but should have been at 103.

I moved up to allow my less experienced teammate to have that spot and benefit the team. By my senior year, I was really pushing my teammates to learn and practice so we could win as a whole and not just have individual success. At one tournament, some of my teammates stole from another. The victim out of rage called them a slur. I don't agree with that but they were trying to beat the guy up even though they stole his money. They were POOP JUICE. I intervened and it was not a popular decision. I always believe in doing things right and being fair. I was not going to allow my teammate to be harmed in my presence. Excellence is a choice. So, in practice the next day, my 160lb teammate was not doing drills and goofing off. I became irritated and demanded he participate. He stood his ground and was being disrespectful, so I mushed him.

This was a POOP JUICE decision that could have cost me my life. I guess this little 135lb frame put fear in the guy. I wanted to fight but you didn't always get that option back then, and especially nowadays. He didn't want to fight little ol' me because he ran out of the gym screaming he would be back. He definitely came back but not alone! He ran up to me with a sawed-off shotgun and fire and anger in his eyes. He looked totally possessed. The basketball team was in the hallway and followed him into the wrestling room, which was the cafeteria. It was as if they wanted to see who he was going to kill.

He shouted at me in front of everyone with the sawed-off shotgun pointed at my chest, "Talk your zhit now, Zoke, talk your zhit now," with rage in his voice. I looked him in the eye and said, "Why would I do that with a gun pointed at me?" I did not flinch. He said, "That's what I thought," and then just left. Everyone was stunned and amazed that I didn't react in fear. They were also giving me POOP JUICE advice. They said that if it was them, they would beat him up or kill him for that. I knew it was all a bluff from them. They would have been crying, begging for their lives, and zhitting their pants. If I followed their advice of beating him up, you would think this time he would pull the trigger. Of course, their other suggestion would land me in prison for murder. I am a fighter, not a killer. This book surely wouldn't be written and my purpose in life would have been unfulfilled. The thought of it gives me chills today. One POOP JUICE decision can cost you everything.

It was a long walk home that day, and when I opened the door, I collapsed in tears. I imagined if he pulled that trigger, I would have been taken from my loved ones and all my dreams would have faded away in an instant. I also thought at the time I just might have gone to hell. My mind was everywhere. What am I going to do? What is it going to be like when I see this guy again? I was thinking that just because someone is disrespectful doesn't mean you should jump in the same zhit they are in. Avoid the POOP JUICE at all costs because if you don't, your life may just be on the line. You never know what people are going through. I chose an EXCELLENT way to handle the situation. I decided to forgive him and it relieved me of the stress immediately. Over the next couple of days, I avoided conversations about it because it was the talk and I was not going to feed it. A couple of days later, he came and apologized and I accepted it. I just never got too close after but revenge would have been a POOP JUICE decision.

Although I dominated my senior wrestling season, I lost at districts to someone I beat easily two times before. POOP JUICE! I was the 2nd seed and lost to a 10th seed. I still hate that memory. All I had to do was stand up. I felt like POOP JUICE and I guess you could say I choked. Nevertheless, I was an all-star who had a bad day on the wrong day.

The track coach always watched me run and invited me to join the team for three years. In my senior year, I finally did. I ran the 800 and the mile. I quickly became known and was winning most races. I had a challenge to beat the number one guy in the county from Penns Grove—a rival city. He beat me in our head-up match. Then I faced him in three straight championship tournaments. He won two. I came in second both times with him edging me out with 6'3" long strides. I was so angry and determined to beat him that, finally, I did in the State Championships. I didn't win the chip but I beat him and that was the chip for me. Actually, I wish I would have listened and started running as a freshman. Funny how those older and wiser tell us things that can help us if we listen. How many of us have lost out on an opportunity because we were hard-headed? It is definitely wise to listen to our successful elders. They have already been where we want to go. Excellent coaching can help us all shortcut our learning processes and overcome POOP

JUICE performance faster than we can on our own—in most cases, not all.

CHAPTER 4

90 DAYS OF EXTREME EFFORT = EXCELLENCE

I learned a secret during my high school years, and it was that anyone who is willing to mindfully focus extreme action with expectation for at least 90 days, can go from POOP JUICE to excellent.

I know this because not only did I excel when I did it, but my friends also did some miraculous things. We would all compete at everything, but I noticed that we could become excellent at things over a short period of time. We all became excellent performers in things we had no clue about before trying, like hunting, tennis, bowling, pool, video games, etc.

Out of the blue one day, we decided to hunt rabbits with nothing but rocks and bottles—never having done anything like that before. We were horrible, it was like a cartoon, we surrounded our first rabbit and all threw at the same time and hit each other in the legs. I can still remember the pain. Ouch!

Never accepting failure, we started going out with mindful, determined action. Once we got one, we would repeat the strategy and it would become easier and easier. Finally, we could feed multiple families if we had to. Of course, people did not believe we could kill wild rabbits with sticks, stones, and bottles, but we believed! To top that, we did it on an excellent level in less than 90 days.

After we would master one thing, we were on to the next. I can remember going to the bowling alley and watching pros bowl 200 and above on average. My friends and I wanted to do it. So, for the next 90 days or so, we did nothing but bowl. We were all POOP JUICE and started out not even scoring 100. We had so many gutter balls that we needed the bumpers. We were bowling daily for hours. Making months' worth of mistakes in just days. We eventually did some things right and, when we did, we were able to repeat it. We learned how to spin the ball without our thumbs after many failures. Then we learned how to pick up spares, then strikes. Once we learned what worked, we did something simple. We repeated it. Sounds easy, but only if you are paying attention all the time.

When you do something that doesn't work, you leave it alone, and with every new try, you stay mindful of all you do. If it works, record and repeat. Once successful, it would not be luck because what you do once, you can do again. That there is a priceless, EZ way to excellence!

Being mindful and focused on every movement and feeling in every right action will help you to remember. You just cannot haphazardly do things and hope to progress!

You must believe without a shadow of a doubt that what is done once, can be repeated!

A really focused person might only need one successful action to become a master. But in most cases, true mastery comes from consistent mindful effort. This focus and drive to do better, paired with consistent action, will always yield excellent results. With this experience in bowling, we were bowling 200 plus regularly after a couple of months. I even bowled nine strikes in a row! Know this... when your heart is set on something, you cannot help but to excel.

When you associate with like minds, you become unstoppable. It definitely helps to have positive peers around you who believe in you, even when competing against each other. The constant eyes keep you sharp, but if you're alone, make it happen anyway.

After I excelled at bowling, I set another goal. Next, I became a pool shark in less than 90 days and was able to run the table often. Why? Because at one point, I did something right and remembered and repeated it. I played so many games in such a short time, my mind was able to process things and my body developed muscle memory because that's all it was focused on. It was so much pressure to win because my friends would run you into the ground with laughter if you were the loser. This gave me the added fuel I needed for my brain to have optimal focus.

I don't play video games anymore, but at one time in my life, that was all I did. If I ever lost at a game, I would stay up all night and play, being mindful of everything I did, and remembering how I lost. After hours of this, I would be unbeatable. Years later, I actually won a trophy in a Bill Walsh 95 tournament in college! My roommates and others in the dorm thought I was crazy, but because I had put in so much focused attention, my brain was able to compute faster and more effectively than my competition. Just know that when you compound your efforts, focus, and drive in 90 days, you will achieve massive results in a short time.

CHAPTER 5

YOU HAVE TO SEE IT AND BELIEVE IT

"Imagination is more important than knowledge. For knowledge is limited, whereas imagination embraces the entire world, stimulating progress, giving birth to evolution."

-Albert Einstein

I have a powerful imagination and you do too. All things we see come from the imagination of another. I have never won anything without winning it in my mind first. You have to take time to focus, where you just close your eyes and visualize yourself accomplishing your goal and being still in the moment. It's the greatest gift you can give yourself. By setting a clear picture in your mind daily, you begin the process of manifestation. But the power comes when you tap into the feeling of accomplishing what you see. This feeling is to be carried with you throughout your day and will lead you in the direction needed to make it happen in real-time. Day after day, your beliefs and expectations build because of the constant picture held in your mind, and you living in the feeling of your goals revealed.

Once you see it clearly in your imagination, you now have a reference point to make it real. Once you have won in your mind or reality, you now and forever will have reference points that will always give you the encouragement and confidence to take on the challenges life will bring. You can build confidence through others' experiences, trusting that if they did it, surely you can too.

I love the story of David and Goliath and how David, before he killed Goliath, had convinced himself and others that just like the bear and lion he killed, Goliath would be no different. David visualized past victories to give him the confidence to visualize his future victory. He believed, and it moved him to conquer the challenge before him.

You are capable of anything. To add to your confidence, just flash back to a time you won or accomplished anything. The most powerful thing I find is how you can see something in your mind, and if you believe it enough, it will happen in reality after you have put the proper work in.

Like with college, I always saw myself going and majoring in business. I then became the first to attend a four-year university in my family. At college, I would meet people from all over the country. I found out early that everyone competes in some form or another and I was determined to represent myself and my hometown well.

Everyone on campus played basketball on the hill and they had a flag football league. They also had pool tables and ping pong in Marcus Foster, which was the rec center at Cheyney University. These things were done on the daily. Before participating, I did something most didn't do. I visualized only winning and used the many reference points in my past to give me the confidence to put into action what I saw in my mind, just like I had previously done with my friends for countless hours. I quickly won a championship in the flag league and was dominant in Marcus Foster also. In my mind, the other students had not put in the work I previously did, so I had such an expectation that it powered me to victory the majority of the time.

The power in everything all begins and ends in the mind. You must be able to truly see and feel what it is that you want, and believe without a shadow of a doubt you can do it. Then, above all else, work past your fears to make things happen.

CHAPTER 6

ANOTHER MOMENT IN TIME

During my second year at Cheyney, I would make another life-changing decision. It only takes a moment in time to change the direction of your life. Some take a lifetime for what can be done in a couple of months or a moment. In 134 Yarnall Hall, I dedicated my life to love and began an all-out love fest for all people. Spirituality helped me see what it truly was to be an excellent human being.

I became like a child and read the whole bible in a week and a half, parts of the Quran and other religious books, and understood more than I ever had. I began the habit of reading and praying daily, which helped keep me on track. Whatever the word said, I believed and did. I'm glad my mother explained to me how to read the new testament because I started from the beginning and, oh boy, there are many laws that made you unclean. I was all in, cold turkey. No more cursing, and previously, I cursed like a sailor. No more sex. I quit cold turkey during the glorious college years, surrounded by temptation, but believed greater is he that is in me than what was around me. I stayed celibate for over five-plus years while walking the straight and narrow path. I really began to do things with all my heart, and later the following year, with the help of my friend, Maurice, we started Ambassadors for Christ Organization!

This organization was very active on campus and became known pretty quickly because of our devotion. We went everywhere and talked to people from home, college, and in the city. I would share the gospel and a message of love with everyone. Soon, many people were following me to my place of worship and coming to hear me speak. I believed that I was empowered to show love and many lives were forever impacted. I made so many friends and learned so much about people and myself just by listening to their struggles and sharing a message of hope.

You reap what you sow

Most people I knew at school, regardless of their religious background, showed me love because I showed them love, and to this day, I still receive testimonies from those who later bettered their lives after they got away from the great temptations that surround you on a campus. Being a servant and helping others, no matter who they are, gives you such a great feeling of fulfillment and is an excellent way to live. You will always hear most people say they are working on their vices and trying to stop what causes them and others harm. What separates those that try and those that stop cold turkey? Simple belief that you can and sincerely want to. Without those two things, you will be trying whatever forever. Most give credit to God and say they couldn't do it without him. Others blame the Devil for the reason they can't do or did something negative.

So, everything is God or the Devil! It is laughable and insincere. A lot of people just say it out of habit, and because it's what the culture teaches, they believe it. It would be more sincere to say they themselves are God and the Devil at any given moment. Taking responsibility empowers you. As a man thinks, so is he. Nothing is impossible to him that believes. The power/spirit is within you, and if you believe that, you know you can do all things through the God/power/spirit within. I, myself, and a lot of others stop many things cold turkey and don't turn all things into a long process. How many times have you heard someone or yourself say, "I'm working on it," and it has been years or months? They or yourself have made working on vices a lifestyle rather than getting rid of them. I believe that they or you enjoy them more than you believe they will have a negative effect on you in the future. The truth is, and proven a million times over, it only takes a moment. One decision with a belief you can, can stop your pain and change your life for the better now rather than later. To put it off is POOP JUICE, and to make up your mind to do it now is the definition of excellence. Your results are entirely up to you. I found that anyone who blames anything outside of him/herself for their life conditions, victories, and failures is not to be trusted. They look outside themselves, which takes responsibility from themselves and this very thing will keep them from rising to their higher selves and maintaining their POOP JUICE disposition. Outside of rare events you have no control over, it is always YOU AND YOUR RESPONSIBILITY to do what is necessary to change your present circumstances.

CHAPTER 7

SPORTS REVISITED

While at Cheyney, I had the opportunity of walking onto the football and wrestling teams. I made the wrestling team, but my shoulder kept dislocating and slowed my progress. I was above .500 but nothing excellent. I was undefeated in my dorm room UFC-style fights and wrestling matches, but I guess that doesn't count.

After not getting a chance to play from 1995 to 1998 due to camp restrictions. The first year I was a Prop 48, which means I didn't score high on my SAT. I was POOP JUICE.

With the SAT, I only took it once and fell asleep during the test. Not focusing and winging it caused me to have to sit out the first year. Not taking the test over was really a POOP JUICE move and I paid dearly for it. It took four years for me to be able to walk on the football team, and I seemed to be at square one again. Luckily, I had reference points that gave me the confidence that even after four years away from the game, I would again do excellent.

For some reason, they treated me like I was POOP JUICE after being away from the game for so long. I was on the third or fourth string to start, and one day, they were making fun of all first-year players. They had us on a stage showing whatever talent we had and making fools of ourselves.

I showed my talent of speaking things that are not as though they are. I told them I would be the captain of the team and starter by the beginning of the season. Of course, they laughed. I was only 148-155lbs and I played Safety. Again, with the same recipe, I spoke my goal publicly, visualized success, and immediately started working with all I had. I began to go all-out on the practice field, hitting anyone and everyone. One practice, I had to go head up with a 230lbs full back and everyone was watching. I could feel my body shivering with tears in my eyes as my fight or flight system began to kick in. I would not be embarrassed, and after the whistle, I destroyed him and just walked to the back of the line. How did I use my fight or flight nervous system to overcome the obstacle before me? I allowed the fear of failing or fear of embarrassment to cause my nervous system to freak out, but I controlled the energy to fight, and when you fight with your life-or-death system in operation, you can do what otherwise might seem impossible. When you speak things and mean it, especially in front of others, you are applying the internal pressure needed to make sure it happens.

Normally, 230lbs beats 150lbs easily, except when one is using his secret power and the other has no knowledge of it or how to trigger it in himself. For me, it was always easy to trigger my fight or flight and use it to my advantage. When faced with huge obstacles that would make me look like a liar if I were to lose, I used this power. This power pushed me to have laser focus and strength in the most crucial of times, while involved in just about anything.

It will always feel so amazing when you walk in the reality of a goal achieved. By the first game against Delaware State, I was the starting strong Safety and middle linebacker on goal line defense at 150 pounds and a captain. I led the prayer before the game and had like 12 tackles before I dislocated my shoulder once again, and my football career shortly came to an end. I was heartbroken because I was always told that I would be injury prone due to my crazy style of play and I still don't want to accept that as true. Disappointed and mad at God, I left the team and began to dream.

CHAPTER 8

YOU MUST SPEAK, BELIEVE, WORK, THEN ACHIEVE

I am going to make the basketball team, is what I told everyone. Of course, they all laughed, which always fuels my fire. Now I'm implementing the same recipe for success towards basketball. Knowing I can do anything, I proclaimed, "I will make the team."

To do this, I would use what I learned with my friends back home. I had reference points. In just 90 days, I transformed into a college-level basketball player having never played in pee wee or high school. I spent hours visualizing, dribbling, shooting, and basket-making day in and day out, while being mindful of every movement needed to succeed. When I came home on break, everyone was astonished at my ability because all they associated me with was football and wrestling, not basketball.

I never played organized ball as a kid. When I tried, I was not good at all. But I was determined to excel—not just in one sport, but many. So, I proclaimed myself a college basketball player. I had a burning desire and a want to be great. I had no doubt that nothing was impossible and got to work to prove my faith.

Oh, how I enjoyed killing all my friends that I grew up with in the game. I told them I was going to play in college and, of course, they did not believe it because I never played in high school. Like most, they feel their past equals the future. But, I spoke things that were not as though they were. They came to pass because I was willing to pay the price to be excellent and go through those grueling 90 days of focused training.

In 1999, I tried out and walked on the Cheyney University basketball team! What an achievement!

With no previous organized experience, I made a college basketball team. That's excellence!

Once on the team, I realized I had a lot to learn. It was rough when I first started. My knowledge of the game was POOP JUICE. I didn't know what the low or high post was or a curl or a cut. The whole thing was all foreign and I was lost during drills. Some of my teammates got a kick out of sending me to the wrong spot on the floor. Within 90 days, I had the fundamentals down and, finally, was comfortable with the flow of the game, right after the Christmas break.

Before the season started, I led the team in our scrimmage scoring while only playing around eight minutes and not knowing much of the game. I scored 18 points. I remember it like it was yesterday. My first shot was an air ball, then six three-pointers followed. I thought I would be a star.

Unfortunately, I had a coach that did not respect the sowing and reaping principles. Anyone in their right mind would figure out how to use someone who is instant offense when in the game. He said he was going to play his All Americans 38 minutes a game during camp. I thought when he saw me on the court it would change his preset mind, but it didn't. The next scrimmage, I had nine in just five min. I worked out tirelessly on my game during and after practice. I was not a starter for the first time since 1988 and was a couple of guards down the bench.

My first home game appearance was embarrassing and an example of excellence at the same time. The team was up a little and the crowd was chanting my name like I was Rudy, but yelling, "Ezell! Ezell! Ezell!"

They had signs in the crowd, "Ezell316". They were showing me love because that's all I gave on campus. I was reaping what I sowed, but not on the team just yet. Finally, the coach called my name and the crowd went wild. As I was checking in, the other team said, "They really love you but we can't let you score." As soon as I got in the game, the ball came to me and I pump-faked their shot blocker and the crowd went wild. I was hyped, shot the ball, and missed everything, "Aiirrrr baalllll". The crowd started laughing. The next trip, I thought I should dunk the ball on the break, but tried a lay-up instead to make sure I scored. My shot was pinned to the glass and, oh my, the cheers turned into hysterical laughter and jeers. My opponent screamed in my face, "NEEEVEERRRR!" In my mind, the coach was feeling justified for having me on the bench but I kept playing. I got the ball again, drove to the left side of the basket, shot the ball, and hit the side of the glass because the same guy that blocked my shot earlier tipped the ball. He was serious about me not scoring. Can you imagine how loud the crowd was? Now my teammates stopped passing me the ball to save me from further embarrassment. There were four seconds left on the clock and I was so determined to score that when the other team tried to hold the ball to end the game, I ran up and punched the ball out of his hands. I took a dribble, went up for a final shot, and the same guy tried to block it again. I faded back and made the shot at the buzzer! We were already winning the game but it still was pandemonium! The gym went crazy and rushed to the floor, screaming, "EZELL! EZELL! EZELL!" Many were screaming,

"You NEVER gave up!" and carried me away like we won the championship. That moment is everything this book is about. Teaching that no matter how POOP JUICE you are, you can become excellent if you know what you want and fight for it and never give up until you get it.

Persistence is one of your superpowers. I know I was being watched like a hawk the whole time on campus because of my love walk, and for them to see me in a very difficult space but yet persevere, really inspired them. I did not have experience and was not the best, but I surely was the hardest worker on the team and should have been rewarded with playing time. I was a freshman on the court but a senior in school on a team with two other outstanding senior All PSAC 1000 point scorers in my position. We had a great team, and if my coach would have used me to do what I did best, we would have won it all.

I played sparingly throughout the season and scored my season high—14 points in six min—which was the longest time I got to play. We were losing by 18, and within three minutes, I scored 10 points and we were down only 8. Coach didn't seem like he wanted us to have a chance because he told us not to foul, which, to us, meant he wanted to lose to prove a point to the starters. I always kept a great attitude, continued working hard every day, supported my teammates, and thought I was going to get my chance to start. Excellence is not easy and walking a faith walk while struggling to find your way is even harder. I never broke character, even when the coach teased me and the team with me starting.

After Christmas break, I had caught on and was ready to explode for 30 when given the chance. During the break, a lot of teammates were late or missed practice altogether, and I never did while still killing it during scrimmages.

Before our game in South Carolina, the coach made a speech that I will never forget. Only one player did everything asked of him during this break and that was Ezell Barnes. I earned playing time. The team got hyped for me and said this was my chance, since most were thinking I was going to start. We warmed up and came back in, and for the first time ever, the coach had written who was starting on the chalkboard. My name was not there and I was devastated. Some of my teammates felt my pain. I felt like he was purposely playing mental games with me. In the moment, I chose excellence and did not respond or act out. I cheered my team on and only got in the game when the starter fouled out. I was delighted and played hard and got on the scoreboard multiple times, very quickly.

Starting a game never happened, but I did win the most improved award at the banquet in my first ever year of playing organized basketball in college. It was bittersweet to win because the trophy had another teammate's name on it. Wow, so I wasn't even the coach's first choice, but I know I was the most deserving of the award and did receive the award gladly. Nothing is impossible! I came in knowing nothing and willed myself into a very good player right before their eyes. What great memories! Even with the character testing I had on the team, it's still evident that extreme effort pushes you toward excellence.

CHAPTER 9

KEEP THOSE THAT BELIEVE IN YOU AROUND!

My good friend, Tonya, who is now my wife, and was a Hall of Fame girls basketball player at Cheyney, worked out with me. She even witnessed me hit eight straight baskets from half-court and many other feats that year. Tonya believed in my potential, so after I graduated, she told me about an overseas pro basketball camp and paid for me to go. It was crazy how I never played basketball until my senior year in college, and now I was going to try out to be a pro. Sometimes, other people's faith in you can drive you to do things that you may not do on your own. I went to the camp, played against division 1 and 2 college stars, and held my own. They invited me to the next camp for free and I did everything right.

I performed at a very high level in front of NBA's Champion and coach, Mo Cheeks, who said I was on the right track and gave me props. Wow... props from someone who was top in this basketball world that I just entered a year ago. No one knew that but me. It empowered me.

I was signed to RGI and played ball in Finland and Estonia/Saint Petersburg, averaging double figures in 20 min or less each game against The A-League Top Pros. I used the same recipe that I used in everything I excelled at before. Although I lacked experience, I visualized myself as a seasoned veteran and meditated on the image so much that I was able to perform as such. Our first game in Finland was tough and we were behind. Although it was a high-pressure atmosphere, I calmly made big plays down the stretch to help pull off the win. I played well in all my games and learned so much in a short time. I am glad I was previously a football player and wrestler because it was very physical, which I don't mind at all. It wasn't uncommon to leave a game with a bloody nose from intentional elbows. I just wiped it off and got back in the game. What an experience.

I was able to see how people from the other side of the world lived and was very thankful for my life in the United States. You were either rich or poor in Estonia. I watched whole families share a happy meal. I returned home and played sparingly in the EBA. I am forever grateful that Tonya believed in me enough to sign me up for a pro camp that allowed me to see a different part of the world. It is amazing how things happen when your whole heart is set on a goal and you are willing to work however long or hard to achieve it. After one year of playing basketball, my work ethic, skills, and vision had me seeing the world.

CHAPTER 10

SAME RECIPE FOR SUPER ATHLETIC GAINS

Now I was going to make a run for the NBA. I found out that they love those who dunk. So, I said out loud, "I am a great dunker," and I started visualizing myself dunking all day. I started working out and making attempts to do what I saw in my mind. Within 90 days, I finished a jump program that would allow me to do any dunk except between the legs. I'm a 5'8.5 guy who could barely touch the rim in high school.

The program involved thousands of jumps by week 12. The increase in strength and stamina from week 1 to week 12 was amazing. I started with a 32-inch vertical and ended with a running 41-inch vertical. Wow!

A few weeks after finishing the program, I dunked on my boy, Porter, who still refutes this story, but he was just the first of many. My 40 speed went from 4.6 to 4.4 unofficially, and this was at 24 years of age. These are dramatic increases that draw a lot of attention. I was so excited and flattered that the POOP JUICE performers thought I was on steroids because of my sudden ability. I took that as a compliment. I also found out that those with dumpster beliefs would rather you be gifted from God than to excel because of hard work. That would mean that they could do it too, and it's like a slap in their face since they are unwilling to work hard and apply themselves. I smacked them all the time! I am no greater than you, and excellence is not just for a few but available to all who are willing to pay the price and follow the EXCELLENT recipe I use for everything.

I always found that concentrated effort allows you to excel, and doing too much at the same time is counterproductive.

After a couple of different camps, I really felt like I was going to make it to the league. I had the bad habit of playing a lot of pick-up games with reckless players, which made me susceptible to injury. Unfortunately, during a game, a teammate dove on me and I severely sprained my knee and tore up my ankle. Before the injury, the kids would wear me out, asking me to do dunks. I would routinely run and do a different dunk on all six baskets in the center I worked out in. They loved it and would use reverse psychology to get me to do it. They would say, "You can't dunk this one," and I would always take the challenge just to entertain them. I just loved doing something most thought was impossible. The injury was heartbreaking, and at the same time, I needed money so I made a pivot into business, figuring I could still become a millionaire if I applied the same principles/recipe I had in sports and spirituality.

CHAPTER 11

BUSINESS EXCELLENCE!

Making the choice to serve and love others in college helped me become a better person by loving and accepting all types of different people. This would help me in my new career path. In April 2001, I took a part-time independent contractor position at Catamount Enterprises, selling Rainbow Air treatment home cleaning systems. I was sold after seeing the presentation and believed it could help solve some of the pollution and filth problems that people have and don't know about. I also like the fact that I could earn as much as I was willing to work for, knowing that "you reap what you sow," and could make my own schedule.

I won my first contest the very first week in the business by setting up the most personal appointments. While I was setting these appointments, I was again met with dumpster juice beliefs! They all said, "You can't make money doing that," and laughed at me because they thought I should be doing something else. "You went to school and you are doing this?"

They mocked me and asked, "Why aren't you playing basketball?" Wow, now they believe in me playing basketball. People, I tell you. It doesn't matter what they think or say, it only matters what you think and what you believe! I received a nice briefcase for winning the contest and my career began. I took the information I was given and began my 90-day transformation. I read the short demo book more than 20 times in the first two days. Most would say that is excessive, but those that are excellent would say it was necessary. I did everything they told me to do to be successful. I also bought books on sales and human behavior. I needed to educate myself in every area that I would be dealing with in this people-oriented career I was taking on. Always be willing to invest in yourself! My first paycheck was $1380.00 for around 20 hours of work. That was more than my father ever made in one week and he had done well for himself, taking care of us. As a son, I felt especially great because he encouraged me during this time.

The company had raises set up if you could reach 10 sales in a month. So, 10 sales was my first goal. I sold eight in May, eight in June, and 13 in July. I was ranked second in the office that month, got my raise, but did not like the feeling of being second place. The next month, I sold 29, becoming a regional sales champion and ranking number one out of hundreds of people, selling over 60%! I would be #1 in the office from that point on.

After three years, I opened my own office for Eagle Eye Enterprises. This fulfilled my dream of having my own business. I quickly became the top area distributor in the region, winning the award many times over. At one time, I had 25 reps selling for me, but I could out-sell them all combined because of my passion and deep belief in my product and myself. After a few years, I had a disagreement with my wholesaler and decided I was not buying any more Rainbows to spite them. Then I hit rock bottom.

I had begun to develop a negative view of the business and dumpster juice beliefs allowed for POOP JUICE performance. Later, I tried to get back into it but I was no longer selling like I was used to. I was not even getting the chance. I would say to myself that the customer would not be home when I got there and, miraculously, I was right over and over again. I would tell some of my partners, "I told you they were going to stand me up." I was using the power of belief in my words in the wrong POOP JUICE direction. So, I would just go play basketball and beat everyone on the court, which would always make me feel better.

I had promised my nephew when he was 16 that I would buy him a car. Well, the time came and he was about to get his license and I had no money. He looked me in the eye and said, "Uncle, you used to be the best, you better get back to your first love."

Hearing my nephew reference me in better times inspired change. So, again, in a moment, I made a decision to go all-out for 90 days and remember my first love and the positivity I started with. That was the last week of August 2006. In September, I sold 21 Rainbows out of 24 presentations. I won both a regional sales championship and an area distributor sales championship at the same time. I did this after not selling anything for months. It felt so good to help my nephew with that car.

Being excellent was so much better than being POOP JUICE. From September to December, I went from zero dollars to over $100,000 doing what people said I couldn't do.

In 2008, the Great Recession began and everyone told me to leave the business because no one would be able to buy. I believed differently, and in February, I sold 30 Rainbows on 38 attempts for a world-best 80% for those over 25 demos and number two in the world on sales. The first-place guy sold one more than me but it took him over 70 shows—double what I had done. So much for the recession.

Most considered me the best in the world. At the regional conference, they asked me what my secret was. I told them just like I will tell you now. I would read the customer's name and, in my head, tell them I loved them and that they loved me, all before even knocking on their door. I am love-driven and people are attracted to that when it's authentic. Also, just like in everything, once something works, I simply repeat the process and the results repeat the same.

To be excellent, you just need to be mindful when doing the right things, remember, and repeat. You really do reap what you sow, not what others think. I not only ran my own office, but I also motivated and helped train every individual that came into the business. Together, the Catamount organization won the King of Year award—the best organization in the world. I helped push this Rainbow organization close to eight figures. I was a main ingredient in pushing an organization to close to 10 million dollars. Feeling and reflecting on that gave me additional faith that I could do the same for myself.

CHAPTER 12

ONLY TAKE ADVICE FROM THE BEST!

I met a multi-millionaire during a Rainbow meeting. He told me and a group of distributors to buy a book called "The Greatest Salesman in the World", written by Og Mandino. I advise you to do the same. I don't think anyone other than myself did. He advised that we read the book and do exactly what it says when it comes to the three-times-a-day reading exercises. It will take like 10 months of your life, but the habits developed will help you not only be a great person, but also give you the keys to extreme success. The book kind of mirrored the ancient principles I already followed but added even more understanding.

The fact that I know most won't follow through, I will quote the second scroll here and advise you to read it three times a day for a month—morning, mid-day, and night. This scroll and the ones that followed definitely helped me become #1 in the world in my field and made me a person of influence. Great for all, but for entrepreneurs, this is a must! Go and purchase it ASAP!

The Scroll Marked II

The Greatest Salesman in the World, written by Og Mandino.

"I will greet this day with love in my heart. For this is the greatest secret to success in all ventures. Muscle can split a shield and even destroy life but the unseen power of love can open the hearts of men and until I master this art I will remain no more than a peddler in the marketplace. I will make love my greatest weapon and none on whom I call can defend against its force.

My reasoning they may counter, my speech they may distrust; my apparel they may disapprove; my face they may reject; and even my bargains may cause them suspicion; yet my love will melt all hearts liken to the sun whose rays soften the coldest clay.

I will greet this day with love in my heart.

And how will I do this? Henceforth I will look on all things with love and I will be born again. I will love the sun for it warms my bones; yet I will love the rain for it cleanses my spirit. I will love the light for it shows me the way; yet I will love the darkness for it shows me the stars. I will welcome happiness for it enlarges my heart; yet I will endure sadness for it opens my soul. I will acknowledge rewards for they are my due; yet I will welcome obstacles for they are my challenge. I will greet this day with love in my heart.

And how will I speak? I will laud mine enemies and they will become friends. I will encourage my friends and they will become brothers. Always will I dig for reasons to applaud, never will I scratch for excuses to gossip. When I am tempted to criticize I will bite on my tongue, when I am moved to praise I will shout from the roofs.

Is it not so that birds, the wind, the sea and all nature speak with the music of praise for their creator? Cannot I speak with the same music to his children? Henceforth I will remember this secret and it will change my life.

I will greet this day with love in my heart.

And how will I act? I will love all manners of men for each has qualities to be admired even though they are hidden. With love I will tear down the wall of suspicion they have built round their hearts and in its place will I build bridges so that my love may enter their souls.

I will love the ambitious because they can inspire me, I will love the failure for they can teach me. I will love the kings for they are but human, I will love the poor for they are so many, I will love the young for the faith they hold, I will love the old for the wisdom they share. I will love the beautiful for their eyes of sadness, I will love the ugly for their souls of peace.

I will greet this day with love in my heart.

But how will I react to the actions of others? With love. For just as love is my weapon to open the hearts of men, love is also my shield to repulse the arrows of hate and the spears of anger. Adversity and discouragement will beat against my new shield and become as the softest of rains. My shield will protect me in the marketplace and sustain me when I am alone. It will uplift me in moments of despair yet it will calm me in time of exultation. It will become stronger and more protective with use until one day I will cast aside and walk unencumbered among all manners of Men, when I do, my name will be raised high on the pyramid of life.

I will greet this day with love in my heart.

And how will I confront each whom I meet? In only one way. In silence and to myself I will address him and say I love You. Though spoken in silence these words will shine in my eyes, unwrinkle my brow, *bring a smile to my lips, and echo in my voice, and his heart will be opened. And who is there who will say nay to my goods when his heart feels my love?*

I will greet each day with love in my heart.

And most of all I will love myself. For when I do I will zealously inspect all things which enter my body, my mind, my soul, and my heart. Never will I overindulge the request of my flesh, rather I will cherish my body with cleanliness and moderation. Never will I allow my mind to be attracted to evil and despair, rather I will uplift it with the knowledge and wisdom of the ages. Never will I allow my soul to become complacent and satisfied, rather I will feed it with meditation and prayer. Never will I allow my heart to become small and bitter, rather I will share it and it will warm the earth.

I will greet this day with love in my heart. Henceforth will I love all mankind. From this moment all hate is left from my veins for I have no time to hate, only time to love. From this moment I take the first step required to become a man among men. With love I will increase my sales a hundred-fold and become a great Salesman. If I have no other qualities I can succeed with love alone. Without it I will fail though I possess all the knowledge and skills of the world.

I will greet this day with love, and I will succeed."

This was long but, really, read this three times a day and apply all you read and it will change your life in just 30 days after reading it 90 times.

CHAPTER 13

WRITE OUT YOUR LIFE AND RELATIONSHIP GOALS!

Once I learned the importance of not just saying your goals but writing them down, I wrote out my life plan over 20 years ago. Here is a copy of it.

"My life plan is to be an instrument of God's Love! To become wealthy enough to support my family and friends and make as many people's dreams come true (financially, physically, mentally, and spiritually). Being an example of reaping what you sow in a Positive Light!

To master the act of giving a hand up rather than a hand out. To be ever-growing in knowledge and wisdom, sharing what I learn with all who will listen. To encourage people to smile and make people laugh every chance I get, all the years of my life.

I plan to have a supportive and loving wife who I can love and support the same. A wife to share my dreams with and help me achieve them. Once stable, to be able to have children and raise them in the way of the Lord and encourage them to be difference makers and leaders. I plan to show my children the way of excellence through love, and at an early age, implant the principle of sowing and reaping.

I plan to see as many beautiful places the Lord has created as possible, "experiencing life to the fullest".

I plan to grow old with my wife and yet be as healthy as we were when we married. To see my kids grow up and have kids.

As death is a part of life, I plan to be remembered by all who came in contact with me as a person who loved in spite of the hateful world we live in, burnt no bridges throughout his life, cherished friendships and experiences with all people good and bad."

From this plan, my whole life is based and is fulfilled daily. Most likely, I wrote my obituary.

So, while dating, I found myself meeting a lot of nice women and learned a lot about them in a short period of time. We spent many hours talking so that within a 90-day period, I would really know them and they would know me. You will learn a lot when you take genuine interest in others.

I believe in being honest and telling the truth, even when I know it's not what people want to hear. I learned that being goal-oriented and hard-working with a purpose was attractive to women. I became good friends with all I dated, but did not make any commitments because I still was building my dream. I was committed to my purpose. For some reason, most people lie when entertaining the opposite sex, but I really found that by being upfront and open, it allowed for others to be themselves. If you're ever going to make the all-important decision to commit to someone, you need to know who you are committing to, at least as much as you can. I genuinely enjoyed spending time with all my friends.

My friend, Tonya, stood out because she had a peculiar way of showing me she loved me regardless of my situations and was always my biggest cheerleader. She had to be the nicest girl on the planet. She was so nice that sometimes I was skeptical and thought she was too good to be true. She was like one of the guys. Everyone liked her and she did fit the description of my future wife. But initially, I kept her in the friend zone as I did a few others. I was and still am dedicated to my purpose and I know how easily one can get distracted by the opposite sex. Some wise man said, "You will lose money and purpose chasing women, but you will never lose women while you're chasing money or purpose."

I read in a Dale Carnegie book once about sexual transmutation, which is basically harnessing the powerful sexual energy that motivates men to chase women and transfer it into the pursuit of one's goals. Many amazing things have men done by using this creative energy to create things other than children and relationships. I actually joke about how people would really be on different levels if they were not able to connect with the opposite sex without accomplishing physical and financial goals first. But since it's not mandatory, most settle with POOP JUICE performers.

Males and females would raise their levels physically, financially, and morally if it was the only way to intimacy. Since today's standards are POOP JUICE, most people will never reach the excellent form of themselves. As long as they can have relationships of some form without excellence, they are cool with being POOP JUICE. A POOP JUICE performer made up the term Gold Digger. He was jealous that the best athletes, best singers, best at anything and successful with money, was the one getting all the girls. Instead of becoming the best, he hoodwinked millions of ladies by shaming them for wanting the best for themselves and labeling all who want the top performers as Gold Diggers. It was a smart move because now the POOP JUICE performer can get girls that he doesn't deserve. A lot of females purposely get with POOP JUICE performers to show they love him for his POOP JUICE performing self, and not because he had anything going for himself. This goes against nature itself. But hey, I guess it was a clever way to procreate without bettering yourself.

One should always choose the best candidate and not feel ashamed. Excellence is pressure and not easy but there are benefits to being excellent. Excellence opens doors and brings opportunities to you naturally. Unfortunately, there is a modern war against excellence on many levels. The POOP JUICE performers outnumber the excellent by the millions. They attack celebrities and well-to-do people with their own success. They say things like, "He/she used his/her celebrity status to influence others."

Now people are targeted for being excellent almost like it's a negative thing. POOP JUICE performers have a lot of time on their hands to do everything but work on being excellent. Don't be POOP JUICE, choose excellence. It is always a better way of life. Truth be told, most people love the attention of the opposite sex and some always have had their attention. A sure way to get attention is to pursue greatness/excellence in anything and you will not only be admired but desired. Once you achieve your goals or see a clear path to achieve them, you will always get to choose who you will bring aboard to help finish or build upon what you started. That will require an excellent partner if you are choosing to have one. Focus is everything and must be maintained to keep forward momentum in this excellent way of life.

In 2007, I finally chose which friend I would ask to marry me. It was Tonya, but it took a lot of effort to get her attention after I allowed so much time to pass without making a commitment. It seemed she had accepted the fact that we would be just friends. Day and night, all I did was text her, call her, and tried to spend time with her, but she kept ignoring me. I did not give up—I had tunnel vision. I had a trip to Miami with my friend, Porter, and I could not enjoy the beautiful sites because my mind was set on Tonya. My boy said I ruined the trip, but he was happy because he knew Tonya was a great girl. At the time, I had many friends that were girls and I personally told them I was going after my heart and I would not be communicating in the same way anymore. I had told everyone my goal, so if she refused me, all would know. My friends said I was crazy for that but I was sold out on the task and, eventually, with persistence, I got my girl. Funny, early on she was chasing me for some time and I never thought I would have that challenge, but it is what it is.

Relationships seem to be the #1 goal for most people outside of securing money. The crazy part is, you don't have full control over the matter. To make a relationship work, the other person must have the same goal that you have to create that lifetime security one seeks. When goals are not aligned, a pursuit to control your partner seems to be the undoing of many relationships. ACCEPTANCE is an excellent way to live within a loving relationship. When you accept your partner for who they are and not try to change them, you find that it allows for transparency and removes the strain of pretending. The moment your individual expression is smothered is the moment resentment settles in the mind and turmoil begins.

Most relationships are POOP JUICE because the construct was designed by someone else for someone else. You are individuals, and to be able to express that, you need to make your own construct that fits your unique relationship. It shouldn't look like everyone else's because you're not them. To go from POOP JUICE to excellence requires truthful conversations that will lead to unique vows you both agree on and that you both will gladly uphold. It is funny how I watch people head over heels in love accepting everything about their partner, but after the honeymoon stage is over, they begin to put restraints and try to change small and big things they overlooked because they were being led by their emotions.

Just know a person who changed against their will is of the same mind still and is just going through the motions and that is POOP JUICE! Life is long and people change as they learn and have different experiences. Life's experiences change you over time. It is of the utmost importance to keep communication and transparency between you and your partner. It is your responsibility to keep your partner informed about the constant changes within yourself and or feelings about life and how you desire your interactions with each other to be. Basically, tell them what you want and never make them guess. Guessing is POOP JUICE, reading minds is POOP JUICE, not speaking for fear of hurting feelings is POOP JUICE, making someone do what they don't want to do is POOP JUICE! ONLY clearly communicating what you want and feel with your partner and allowing them to respond how they truly desire and accepting that response can lead to EXCELLENCE.

An atmosphere of truth and acceptance will always give you the best chance of having excellent relationships of any kind. Over 22 years together and 16 years married, my relationship with Tonya has been transparent and I have heard those on the outside have their opinions because we don't look like, act like, or want to be like any other couple. You cannot possibly know or understand one's unique walk. I just encourage others to be real with themselves and create their own construct and not to measure it against anyone else's. It is always best to be different and it is in your differences that you most likely find your peace set aside for the individuals you are. There is no peace in imitating others. You can see things you like in others but only add them to yourself if it resonates with who you are. Tonya and I have managed to stay together through many years of ups and downs during our dream chasing. Poverty brings extra pressure, but if you both have set personal and business goals that you see clearly happening in the future, you are able to get through the struggle. Zuccess is setting goals and actively pursuing them. The idle mind creates problems. Be too busy to be bored. Set many goals together that you both want and spend the rest of your life pursuing them together. This will give you a purpose-driven life. Always remember, it takes two, and at any time, one can choose to change their mind about anything. Change is ok, you just have to pivot, have the conversation, and see if new goals can be established. Sometimes partners switch all the way up and can no longer co-exist. This is ok too. It hurts but you regroup, gather yourself, get over it, and continue to pursue your life's goals.

One thing I don't like to see is fairytale relationships based completely on emotionalism. They are POOP JUICE! These couples' lives are dictated by poetry, novels, and love music. I have seen some success stories but they are few and far between. In real life, I have observed most people suffer unwarranted heartaches. Logic has to play a role in relationships. The first mistake is to believe there is one soulmate for you. Not true. We hope that the first love we have lasts forever, and it is possible, but if it doesn't, please know that there is another person you can be compatible with and you still have your life's goals to pursue.

There are many who become so distraught when the other leaves or passes on, to the point they cannot function or even have no desire to live by themselves. Some are so pathetic that they take everyone out in the name of love and ownership. These are POOP JUICE responses.

I hear others react to these stories and say they want a love like that. Not me, I want you to continue to pursue your goals and be an asset to society no matter your age.

Heartbreak is real and is intensified with our words. We repeat poems and love songs that give us fairytale feelings. Things like, "I can't breathe without you, can't eat without you, can't live without you," actually become a reality to some. I say it is a red flag and not romantic at all for potential mates to verbalize these types of statements to each other. It is important for both partners to have personal goals outside of being with each other. If one or the other becomes your all in all goal, things can become dangerous. You can lose yourself, and when you lose yourself, you've lost. Love is freeing, giving, always building, patient, understanding, and logical, but emotionalized fairytale ownership relationships are illogical, and most end badly with one or both trying to harm the other in some way. In most cases, neither can live up to the lofty standards and fake facade. The self-imposed pressure takes its toll, leaving one or both feeling not at peace and feeling cheated because Romeo is no longer Romeo and Juliet ain't fitting the bill either. These are due to the unrealistic expectations and people not being their true selves. Acceptance is the furthest thing from these relationships once the honeymoon period is over.

There was a time when I wanted to impose my will for certain changes in the household concerning child rearing and business, but after a while, I realized we both had strong beliefs about what we desired and some of those things were in opposition.

Outsiders looking in had strong opinions and told me to put my foot down, but their advice was not applicable because they cannot understand our dynamic, and they're not supposed to. Actually, I shouldn't have been sharing my frustrations with them in the first place. I decided I would look at things from a different perspective and walked in acceptance, and it immediately relieved me of internal stress. The crazy thing is that most of the things being done were for my own benefit, but I wasn't looking at it that way. I have never felt pressure to do anything other than be myself in my partner's presence, and me allowing for the same actually was an excellent decision.

My relationship with my daughter is a special one that could have been strained if I didn't fall back on the not-so-simple subject of bedtime. Although working 130-plus hours a week, my daughter and I have been able to share some hours together every day of her life. This is because of her non-traditional sleeping habits. It was usual for me to come in after midnight, but my daughter would be wide awake waiting for me. I was against this at one point, but see clearly now the bigger picture thanks to the wit of her mother. How much time would I be able to spend with my daughter if she had a normal bedtime? This was a question posed by Tonya that gave me an epiphany. I left my house at 7 am or 8 am and returned around midnight for years, almost every day. So, I still got to read, play, and incorporate my after-hours work, including collaboration videos with my daughter, every day. Her being home-schooled allowed for this.

There are always some things that get compromised, but the way you look at it will determine if you have peace or turmoil. When you find yourself not at ease, make sure to communicate that to your partner, but also evaluate your perspective because a simple change in your view can instantly relieve you. Yes, you get to choose to change your perspective at any time, which will change the way you feel. You can also choose to maintain it and deal with it. Always your choice. Choose wisely.

Choose to have meaningful relationships with others. Always look to build upon or make new connections during our life's journey.

I believe it is important to make new friends and build relationships with others. People are bridges and I act as a bridge for many. The Hip Hop Culture preaches burning bridges and celebrates having no new friends. This ideology cripples the participants and limits their ability to advance in this world. Of course, they can still excel, but the right collaboration can make it easier. When you don't add new relationships, you most likely will stay where you are or decline.

There is a saying that your net income is the average of your five closest friends. If that is true, your income or place in life has a cap according to who you're connected to. New friends in different positions in life will actually help open doors for you. How do I make new friends? It is written that those who want friends must first show themselves to be friendly. Yes, friendships are built upon sharing info, experiences, products, and time. Closed mouths don't get fed is a saying. Introducing yourself and just sharing a little of who you are or just sharing good energy with a smile is a great way to start a new relationship of any kind. Remember, when you lead with love, you are already giving off positive vibes. Others are way more receptive if they don't perceive you as someone who is there to take from them. Always give first, then you may receive. One thing is for sure—over time, it would be great to have built some kind of relationship with those from all walks of life. Have a mechanic, handyman, teacher, preacher, old, young, rich, hood, a computer specialist, business owner, landscaper, realtor, lawyer, doctor, comedian, musician, artist, banker, athlete, counselor, councilman, politician, accountant, police, those with different religious beliefs, adventure seeker, and people from as many different races and cultures as possible. Having these relationships will automatically make your life easier!

CHAPTER 14

GO FROM FAT TO FIT, JUST BE CONSISTENT!

After a few years of marriage, I got fat, like many people do, which is POOP JUICE. Everything was harder to do, even just bending over. Playing ball is not the same when you get tired the first couple of times down the court. Fat is not fun. I was enjoying a successful Rainbow business and marriage and chose not to work out, which did not line up with the life plan I wrote out, which was POOP JUICE! I was laughed at by my mother-in-law after she saw me topless on a cruise. I was embarrassed, so I decided at that moment to change what I was doing. I announced my goal to the world and believed I would do it. In 60 days, I went from 205lbs to 160lbs. I was in my early 30s ripped up like I was in college. Every day, no matter if I was tired or fell asleep, I would wake up and make sure I did my workout. I did not let a day go by where I let my focus slip.

The program I did was Insanity by Shaun T. I also played basketball three to four times a week and this helped me transform in 60 days. You can do the impossible! You do not have to get old and sloppy. If you stay active, you will age so much slower.

Staying consistent in all areas is a huge key to excellence. After you blast off with your 90 days of extreme effort, you will need less effort to carry you toward your dreams and to maintain what you already built. Just like a space shuttle drops its rocket launchers after it gets into the stratosphere where there is less gravity. A space shuttle only needs the regular jets to get anywhere else it needs to go because it's less resistant to excellence! That's why they say the first million is the hardest, then it seems like magic from there.

I admire athletes like Bernard Hopkins because he does not listen to others when they say he is old and should retire. He is a champion going on 50. He consistently outworks and outthinks younger opponents because of his mastery and belief system.

How anyone can see others do great things and feel it is not possible for them is beyond me. I look at YouTube and find people in their 70s still playing ball and lifting weights in better shape than most 20-year-olds. So, I plan on not aging and staying fit, all the while, everyone around me wears away because they buy into dumpster juice beliefs.

Dedicating just 30 mins a day to exercise will keep you healthy and fit. Even doing a consistent workout three times a week will suffice for some. Make sure it is your total body because, if you don't use it, you quickly lose it. I know first-hand how it feels to be tight, stiff, out of breath, and unable to move freely because I chose to neglect myself. Even though I was active all my life, it only took a little over a year of inactivity for me to start aging dramatically.

I recommend you Google workouts to stay fit. Watch YouTube videos of those that inspire you. Also, Google a balanced meal plan. Your diet is very important. I personally always ate junk but was so active, you could not tell. If I had a healthy diet, I wouldn't have gained as much weight so fast. I definitely had a POOP JUICE DIET!

Make a commitment to be consistent, but tell someone so they can hold you accountable. That is why I tell the world, so I not only have my expectations but many others for me to do what I said I would do.

I have learned that, throughout your life, you face challenges, you reach some goals, some you do not, but you learn, you win, you lose, you go up, and you go down.

What is consistent is the dumpster juice beliefs and opinions of those around you. Their disbelief and pessimism stinks like POOP JUICE! Your greatest defense is making up your mind that you and only your opinion matters when it comes to achieving your dreams.

Your vision is just that—it is a bonus when others believe, and you should definitely marry someone who believes in you! I like to share my visions and goals, but it is really not for them to understand. Regardless of their reaction, I must move in the direction of bringing my ideas, dreams, and goals into a reality.

CHAPTER 15

MILLION-DOLLAR IDEA

I had an idea one day while sitting on my couch. I just made a great-looking fish hoagie after Tonya fried some fish. After I tasted it, I immediately thought, wow, this will sell! I told Tonya that we were going to sell fish hoagies. She looked at me in disbelief *(but remember, your ideas and visions were given to you for a reason)*. I have a great wife, so she was going to support me no matter what. The very next day, I called my very opinionated sister over so she could taste it, and to my surprise, she said it was terrific. I knew right there it was going to sell because she hated everything. I needed a name, and after throwing out a few, we came up with "Zoagies - Unbelievable Fried Hoagies."

So, Zoagies began. I went to Walmart to buy my first $40 fryer and supplies. Then I drove to Philly on Wadsworth Ave for some fresh fish. That Saturday, we had a basketball tournament for the championship and we won. I told everyone that I had a new business and invited everyone to try Zoagies in my backyard. I told my team it's the best way to celebrate. I told the losers also to come because there's no greater way to get over a loss than to eat a Zoagie.

One thing is for sure—to start and grow a business, you have to have a product that has demand, and the only one way to find out if the product is good is to get it in front of people and let them try it out. The funny thing is, I have some very opinionated teammates, so when they took their first bite of a Zoagie, I knew they would tell me the truth. Not to my surprise, they raised their eyebrows and said it was pretty good. I knew I just had to evolve, keep pressing, and we'd be able to build something nice.

The hood is a great testing ground for any product. If the hood loves it and likes it, the world is going to also.

In business, an invisible man or woman can't sell a thing no matter how great their product is.

Immediately, word-of-mouth marketing began. Everyone started telling everybody about my backyard business. Word on the street, you had to try a Zoagie. It was going well, but I needed to speed up the process. I decided to go to the people myself, so I rode my bicycle around town, giving out samples. Once people tasted a sample of a Zoagie, they immediately wanted to order. This was spring 2012 and, for some reason, people stayed out until around 5 am. I was hungry and hustling out there every night.

I was really excited and wanted people to know about my business. Plus, we needed money badly. I would stay out between 4 am and 5 am every night going up and down the street delivering Zoagies. If you're going to build a dream or build anything of relevance, you have to work. It takes sacrifice and I was willing to sacrifice sleep and anything else just to make sure I was getting my product out there. At that time, Tonya and I didn't have much knowledge about the food business or where to buy supplies. This had us traveling from state to state daily, going from store to store. After a few months, I announced that I was gonna make this a million-dollar business. I did this even though I wasn't even an official business yet—I had not applied for a business license or anything. I was willing to take the risks to see whether or not there would be enough demand for my product.

It became obvious fairly quickly that Zoagies was something special. I had people coming to me while I was still in my backyard, offering to buy me a food truck so that I could do better. I was not open to taking on any partnerships or deals that were gonna have me share the limited earnings. With me having 100% ownership, there still wasn't much profit yet.

I took every little penny I made and put it back into the business. I tried to pay some bills and found out that Zoagie money wasn't nearly as much as the money I made in my previous profession. Even still, I purchased multiple Walmart fryers until I was finally able to get a commercial tabletop fryer. By the end of summer, I had at least 100 people coming into my backyard, and at that time, I knew I had to become official. Over the winter, I tried to keep business alive but it was very difficult being out there with a tent. During this time, I tried to sell some Rainbows to get through it, but the struggle was real. I never figured out why, as soon as September hits, all of a sudden people didn't want Zoagies. Maybe the blistering cold and wind and rain and sleet and snow was a cause of it. I thought to myself, before the next winter, I'm going to get a food trailer or truck so I can stay open year-round. I also decided that I was no longer going to sell Rainbows. I decided to cut all ties to force myself to succeed because it was my only option. I find a lot of entrepreneurs I know keep their day job until they can afford to do what they dream of. I think there's some wisdom in that, but I'm different. I needed to cut all other options. There was no plan B, no backup plan, no cushion. I am gonna make this work no matter how hard or how long it takes, even if it means losing everything.

I thought, worst-case scenario, I could go back to my mom's house if they take mine or live in my car. Tonya did not even like the thought of it. I can remember telling her I wouldn't be mad if she left me for greener pastures, even though I knew without a doubt it would be a mistake because I was going to figure this out. I was willing to give up everything and I pretty much did. I just forced myself to be in a position that was going to force me to succeed. I was sold!

CHAPTER 16

DIVINE UNIVERSAL FAVOR

A lot of people want things or have certain desires, but it's not until it becomes a burning desire that you're totally sold on, that all of a sudden, it seems like the universe or divine providence takes place. People, places, and things that normally wouldn't come your way, come your way, and events happen that pretty much help you towards obtaining what you want. That first winter was horrible and cold and it was rare to get customers to come out. Money was very funny.

One morning, I woke up to the smell of oil and I was wondering what was going on in my basement. When I checked down there, I found that the entire basement was filled with oil and all my Rainbow trades and vacuum products were ruined. I found out that an oil company made a wrong address delivery. I already didn't have any money, and now me and Tonya were forced to move in with my mother. It was a two-month process to remove the oil, clean it out, and make the grounds and house livable again.

Over those two months, bills piled up. I actually decided to use my Rainbows to start a cleaning service. I reached out to former Rainbow customers and friends. We started cleaning carpets and pissy beds to get some type of income. By now, my credit was trash and I didn't have any provable income to get anything from a bank. Cleaning was POOP JUICE, but we did EXCELLENT work. Boy oh boy, Tonya and I hated it. We had our deals for three rooms for $100. I remember that we would do the stairs and we had to scrub and vacuum the floors to a deep clean using my Rainbow system to get all the dirt out. It was hell and we'd be there for hours to make that $100.

I promoted like crazy and got a lot of biz, but not enough to pay serious bills. I had every offer in the book to go and sell the Rainbows from different distributors. I knew I could make a lot of money doing that, but it would take away my burning desire to make Zoagies successful.

During this time, it was very hard hearing family and friends telling me to get a job. "Get something guaranteed and keep your little business on the side." It was like they were cursing at me. Now I understand that family and friends do love you. Some loved ones actually don't want you to do better than them, so they try to discourage you, but for the most part, they just wanna see you doing well. People around you usually don't see what you see. Your vision is your vision! If you see your vision as clearly as I did, you would know to stick to your guns regardless of them calling me hard-headed or saying I'm going to suffer for the decision. I was willing to. I had faith and no doubt that I had to stick to my guns. They saw a little business that I really didn't know much about, but I saw a multi-million-dollar business. Sometimes, bad things turn out to be good because the insurance company had to cover all of my Rainbow products, so I was able to get a check for around $18,000, which we needed desperately. I used the money to pay some bills, buy a lawn mower trailer, three Cajun fryers, and a tent. It's crazy how that unfortunate event helped me get the equipment I needed to help me become an official business.

CHAPTER 17

OFFICIAL FROM BACK YARD TO UPTOWN

There is a big difference between running a bootleg business out of your yard and running an official business in which you're doing things according to the law.

I definitely was POOP JUICE when it came to knowledge of the food business and what it took to get official licenses, health inspections, and permits. It was really a challenge at first, but of course, I figured it out. You can Google anything in this age and I found out what I needed to do to get a license. I went to the municipal building and asked for the paperwork for licenses and permits to do vending. I also found out I needed to apply for a state business license and a sales and use tax license.

In order to get my Salem city license, I actually had to first get a Salem county health permit, in which my new equipment would have to be set up and inspected for use. I found out that I also had to get a Safe Service Certification, which ensures you know all the ins and outs of proper safety when handling food. I needed to become a certified food handler, which started another process of studying and learning so I could pass the test. I used my same recipe for success that I use with everything else. I studied the material day and night, and after a short period, I knew my stuff and got my certification. I also found out I had to have a commissary, which can be expensive. I talked to an old friend and officially had the 49 Deli as my place to do business in the city. I set up my inspection, got my permit, then went downtown, paid my fee, then I had to wait for a council meeting and for the sheriff to approve my background. There was a lot going on with that process that makes you want to quit, but of course, you gotta do what you have to do. In May 2013, Zoagies became an official business. We immediately started doing business. It was unfortunate that the only place we could do business was at the 49 Deli, so we would have to wait until they closed at 8 o'clock and we would set up to open at 9 pm. We would just go until the people stopped coming. Zoagies had officially started, but didn't have a place to do business during the day except on Sundays, when 49 Deli was closed. We were on the main highway on Broadway, and I thought people passing by would see our establishment and we would grow in popularity quickly, especially on Sundays during the day. But we found out very quickly that in Salem, you cannot vend on Sundays and they shut us down. That left us only open at night. We were doing well at night and sometimes it would get loud, so shortly after we started there, the city said that we would have to be packed up and gone by midnight! Wow, we were really doing something in the city never done before. People loved the late-night food and vibe at Zoagies, especially after the bars and clubs closed. I was so mad that the city was restricting my ability to earn a living to take care of my family. I say family because, at this time, Tonya was pregnant. I've always been frustrated with laws and regulations that restrict business owners from earning a living. I never understood it and never will because it's not right. But the obstacle was there, and if you really want to do something, you figure it out. I have seen many people start a business and find out how many obstacles and restrictions there are and just quit. I had no plan B, and there is no such thing as quit, just learn and adjust. There's a proverb that informs all to do your due diligence before getting into building anything. To do research and count the costs, and find out what is needed to complete whatever you're building. I agree, but I was willing to learn on the fly. I clearly saw myself running and owning a million-dollar business, but I did not know how or what would happen in between getting there. But I was up for it and was willing to go through whatever in order to get there. As they say, trust the process. After a while, things died down at 49 Deli and I had to really figure out how I could get further uptown and try to do business. A friend of mine opened up Smitty's, and he looked out for me. He allowed me to open up my trailer in front of his business and we began doing well again. Me and Tonya were grinding it out until we needed the help of some family. It was something special, and shortly after we started there, a lot of the stores uptown went to the council meetings and complained about Zoagies. At this point, we pretty much got kicked out of my own town.

CHAPTER 18

OUT OF TOWN, LOVE SOCIAL MEDIA REACH

It is said that a prophet is only without honor in his own home, but everywhere else, he will find honor. When starting any business or venture, we will always naturally want those closest to us to be our greatest supporters. Sometimes that is not the case. A lot of times, when you're just starting, it will feel like the very opposite. Your hometown, your friend, your family member can actually seem to be your greatest obstacles. They love you, but it will feel like they blatantly are trying to kill the dream that you have. The longer you listen to POOP JUICE performers, the more likely you will stink also. I spent minimal time with those who didn't mirror my drive or ambition. You really have to almost avoid them like a plague, no matter if they're family, friends, loved ones, it doesn't matter.

If you really want to get where you're going, you can't allow negative energy or anything opposing your goals to feed your spirit. It will drain you and you need all the energy possible to continue to pursue the invisible. They can suck all your motivation if you let them.

Many times, those around you are content with where they are, and you pushing for more can make them uncomfortable. Not everyone is a dream chaser, not everyone is a supporter, not everyone is a game-changer, not everyone is a boss, not everyone is a risk-taker, and that is OK. But if you are an entrepreneur, a dream chaser, and a game-changer, you must put yourself in the presence of only those types of individuals because they are what you want to be and they will support you. Otherwise, you put yourself in a world with which most don't understand and cause yourself friction.

Find where you are celebrated and not tolerated and that will give you so much more peace of mind and give you a foundation to grow from. Some really want you to make it so that they can be encouraged to go for theirs. It is never all hate. I actually believe I got a lot of hometown love, just not enough to get where I am trying to go.

So, you will have to realize some mean well and some don't, but neither has anything to do with you pursuing your goal because there are billions of people ready to be sold!

Over the years, I definitely was using social media to help get the news out about my business. What was funny is that people from our rival town, Penns Grove, New Jersey, would come to Salem to support me. Penns Grove is only about a 15 to 20-minute drive from Salem. But my customers who would come from there always said that if I came to Penns Grove, I'd be treated like a king. The first day I got to Penns Grove, customers were waiting for me and even helped me set up.

From day one, we were popping and they were lined up and down the highway to get Zoagies. I had my little tent and trailer set up on the road and, oh my Zod. I felt love like I had never felt before. I felt like a real official food business. It was consistent business and people appreciated everything that I did. I did something never done before after getting the green light from the city. I would arrive at 10 am, open at 11 am, and would not close until after the bar let out and cleared out around 3 am. I couldn't afford metal cans, so I always had to wait an hour for grease to cool. I would get home around 4 am-4:30 am go to sleep for a couple of hours, get up at 6 am-6:30 am, and drive to Philly to get supplies and get back home around 8 am or 9 am to prep and tell T to bring the rest to the trailer. At 10 am, I'd get there to set up and be ready to start at 11 am. I did that every day while in Penns Grove. I had some help from my nephews and brothers-in-law, but I trained myself not to use the bathroom until I got home because I couldn't leave the trailer by itself. Amazing how your body can adapt when your mind is focused on a task, never even thinking about the bathroom or eating as long as it had work to be done. I'll always have to remember that everyone is not like me and everyone's focus is different. My focus is completely on the people and the work that needs to be done. I had to learn that my family and friends working with me needed to go to the bathroom and they needed to eat. I understand that now, but I didn't for a little while. That was an awesome summer. I learned a lot and Zoagies' name grew.

While in Penns Grove, we had a lot of social media support. People would blast on all their pages that Zoagies was in Penns Grove. I had a good friend of mine named Twitty. He was really popular on social media and helped me out a lot. One day, it actually piqued my mind to create something called Znglish. Twitty came to the trailer and said, "Zoke, let me have a zaco." And I said, "What is that?" He said, "A taco." I said, "Oooh!" and I immediately began to speak with a z in front of some words and realized putting a z in front of a cuss word made it no longer profane. Zish, zhrimp, zrab like you never had, I would regularly say zamn, zitch, and zuck but all would laugh who heard it. So, I put a z in front of all items on the zenu and it became a thing. Znglish is Zoagies' own official language. Unfortunately, after having this great summer in Penns Grove, my six-month permit was up. So, I was back home in the yard trying to figure out what to do next. We opened zveryday but it was very slow. Then, one day, I received a call that I hoped would be my big break.

CHAPTER 19

OPPORTUNITY

I received a call from the manager of the Vineland Amish Market. Vineland New Jersey was about an hour away, and the guy asked me if I would be interested in coming and being a part of the Amish market there. He had an empty kitchen and didn't like it to be empty. He asked me to serve Zoagies because he had heard so much about our unique product. He allowed us to be there free of charge. Only a year and a half in business and Zoagies' name was ringing bells an hour away. I was very excited and accepted the offer. Of course, I needed to do the county and city paperwork, but I did what I had to. Amish markets are usually very busy, so when we got there, we set up our trailer outside and a commercial fryer inside, then started doing business. In the beginning, it was very slow, but after a couple of weeks, we were doing ok. I was doing a lot of social media advertising and it was a steady little pace but not great numbers. I then received a suggestion that could have really been a game-changer but I was unsure of the intentions at the time and a bit suspicious. The manager asked if I would be willing to allow the Amish to run Zoagies. Basically, I'd disappear and let all Amish workers work the business. I seriously thought about it but it kind of felt like a trap. I only felt that way because I had previously created a program at Rainbow, in which I wanted to make residual money in perpetuity. I secured a lawyer, got contracts drawn up, and somehow, that program was still stolen from me, and to this day, I have never made money from it. I kindly told him I was not interested. I later thought about it, and if Zoagies would have done very well there, there would probably be Zoagies in all the Amish markets around the nation. I am a firm believer in forgiving and not punishing people for other people's mistakes, but I also am a believer in learning from mistakes and not falling for the same trap. Imagine Zoagies in all Amish markets and they don't even know who the owner is. I'll never know for sure if this was a missed opportunity. I do know now that whenever you're doing business, your paperwork and contracts have to be tight. A thorough, trustworthy lawyer is a must or you're subject to getting played.

CHAPTER 20

BE ZIFFERENT

What does it mean to be yourself? A lot of people find themselves trying to find themselves as they get older and they take time to meditate, look within, and try to put away what they see as conformity and ask themselves a question: How do I really feel? What do I really think? When you come up with the answer to those questions, you find out you are very different from most, and if you own it, that realization will be your peace and power.

Although the majority of the world conforms to societal norms and their surroundings, it is usually those who are different who stand out and become the leaders and the more successful of our times. If you think about it, it is those who are different who are the celebrities, who are the stars, and who are the radical politicians. It's their differences they celebrate and that is their power.

Don't get me wrong, POOP JUICE individuals will always fight those who don't conform to societal norms, so it is actually a challenge to be yourself in today's society. In order to become excellent, you must be you! You must grab ahold of who you are and don't let yourself go. Your uniqueness is your key to excellence. You are to use your unique ideals, your unique talents, and your unique personality to pave a way to become an asset to society. You automatically stand out because you are different from everyone else, and the way you move will immediately bring attention to yourself—attention that you need to utilize to help fulfill whatever purpose you have. When trying to accomplish any goal, it is very difficult to do things unseen. There are some things done in the dark, but most things need attention for them to get done. An invisible man or a woman cannot sell a thing. A man or woman that doesn't speak up or say anything can never get the mate that they desire. You must get attention at all costs to accomplish the majority of your goals.

I read a book once called The Purple Cow. This was a great read and a great marketing book. The Purple Cow talks about how, if you pass a farm and see cows, you most likely won't say anything about it because you've seen cows all the time. But if you were to pass a farm and see a purple cow, you would immediately tell people there is a purple cow at that farm on that highway because it is zifferent, and something never seen before. It sticks out, which will cause you to open your mouth and bring attention to it.

I believe everyone should be a purple cow because everyone should be different. Unfortunately, most people are not, therefore, if you are, you will definitely stand out.

I made myself a purple cow outside of my personality. I decided to wear a chef hat in all different colors every single day, year after year, until it got to the point where individuals would not recognize me with my hat off. I wore my chef hat to the gym to work out. I wore my chef hat to the basketball court to play basketball. I wore my chef hat to funerals. I wore my chef hat to weddings. I wore my chef hat with everyday clothes. I wore my chef hat to clubs. I even wore my chef hat to bed. I actually wore my chef hat in an official league the whole season. I had people talking no matter where I went. I was keeping their mind on my business, Zoagies, but at the same time, I was promoting myself, setting myself up for future success. The hat always caused people to ask me where I cook or what I do. This immediately gave me a chance to advertise my business, and my business needed to be a purple cow. That's also why I spoke Znglish and I made the product itself a purple cow.

The name of my company is "Zoagies - Unbelievable Fried Hoagies", and this name and statement always piques interest. People would always ask me, "Do you fry the whole thing?" and I would always tell them, "No, we just fry the foods and we use fresh grinder rolls." But while I was in VINELAND at the Amish market, during some slower times, I told myself, if I can fry this roll, it will be a purple cow. It will have a WOW factor, so I became like a scientist and put that roll in the grease, and when I pulled it out, it was greasy as h***. I tried again, and this time, I held it under the grease longer and it came out better, so then I switched the temperature, held it there, and pulled out the roll and it was like a shining, glistening, beautiful golden-brown roll with no grease on it. When I sliced the roll open, the steam came out and I was like, "Wow, this roll is gonna become gold." Since then, Zoagies has become a very, very popular food truck because it's a purple cow. Zoagies is the only food truck where you can come and get a fried roll that tastes so amazing, it never again has to be sold.

Funny, I've always been told that I was different since childhood. My mother would always tell me I was her prayer baby and that I was anointed that I was gonna make a difference in the world. She said that I was going to do great things. I've always carried that in my mind, accepted that I'm different, and accepted who I was. I never expected to be like anyone.

I also saw that a lot of people didn't accept who they are and they conform and act just like everyone else. People have to realize their power is in their uniqueness. It is POOP JUICE to act like someone else to the point where you're not yourself. I believe in seeing things you like in others, taking it from them, and making it your own. I do believe we can learn from everyone and there are things we can take from everyone to add to our own being, and that's what we do. We add, we don't become something else. We are who we are and we add upon that and that is our power. BE ZIFFERENT, IT IS YOUR PATH TO EXCELLENCE!

CHAPTER 21

YOU ARE A PROPHET

There are steps in the process of manifesting your dreams. I believe everything starts with the thought, which then produces an image in our minds. The image or vision we see will cause us to react in two ways. You run with it or you let it go because of your ignorance of what it will take to make it real. To run with it is an excellent decision. The first thing you do is:

1. Speak exactly what you see in your mind.
2. Write it down.
3. Keep the image in the forefront of your mind so you can feel it.
4. Ask yourself a powerful question. How can I do it?

5. Have faith that you will get the answers as you go.

The answers are within you, just like the image came from you. You will be led to research but always be mindful of your inner voice because it is possible we get the answers and not recognize them.

I definitely have prolonged a lot of things that could have been done much sooner if I listened to the answers from within. MOST ANSWERS INVOLVE MASSIVE AMOUNTS OF WORK AND SACRIFICE IN ORDER TO MANIFEST YOUR PROPHESY! Some don't, but I guess I haven't been fortunate to hear those. But I do observe my surroundings enough to know that there is more than one way to make things happen. A good listener might hear the shortcut route. That's why it's important to meditate and be around those who are where you want to be. They already have the answers if your goal is to be where they are. If your vision or goal is something new being added to the world, then you will find the answers as you go from within.

After a couple of months of working at the Amish market, we were back on the street with our trailer tent set up. The struggle was real. I had prophesied months before that I was gonna have a child on Tonya's birthday. I became a proud father on Jan 16, 2014. My baby girl's name is Azalea. She is so beautiful and wise beyond her years! I would speak to her while in the womb, affirming that she would be wise, intelligent, a great decision-maker, loving, discerning, strong, and quick-witted. I continue to speak this to her, along with how beautiful she is. What is awesome is the fact that she is all those things I spoke about before she was even born and after. Prophesy is powerful and speaking things that are not as though they are is really our birthright. We had her according to our plan and vision, in spite of everyone telling us how and what to do during and after pregnancy. I am a product of my mother's prophecy. I was never told I was bad, I was never told that I wasn't good enough, I was never told I will grow up to be a mess, I was never told anything negative, I was only told that I was prayed for, I was here for a purpose, and I would do great things if I would take heed to wisdom.

A lot of those who are POOP JUICE are the victims of their parents speaking negatively. They told babies that they're bad. Told them that they will be like their no-good daddy and they were a mistake. I was young and dumb when I had you, etc. Downloading into their brain low self-worth and a lack of purpose. Some told children that they infringed on their life instead of blessing it. Don't be a doomsday prophet, choose to only speak positively because, either way, it has a high chance of being fulfilled. There will be exceptions, but choose to speak life and positivity. No POOP JUICE! No one has to stay under the power of either positive or negative prophecy of others. We can overcome and become excellent and we also can go from excellent to POOP JUICE. What you speak about yourself is the most powerful factor. The first download comes from parents, family, and friends speaking over children. Guard your children and make sure they're not around those who speak negatively in any way.

When you say or believe things, you have to be disciplined or you may derail your dream. Actions speak louder than words, but they both have impact. I believe highly in discipline and avoided allowing my seed to enter my wife for six years during marriage. That seed went everywhere except for where it was supposed to go. A lot of people thought we were barren because we had no kids and we were 37 and 32 years old. We had to have a problem, they thought, especially because we were not using birth control. When you want something, you will deny yourself to get it, and I wanted to have a child when I wanted to. I predicted Tonya's birthday for the date of birth of my child. Family and friends laughed, "You can't do that," and of course, I said, "Watch me!" I wound up three days off, but you get the point. You can't buy into the hype and opinions of others because, again, only what you think matters in this world. You can create the world you choose rather than just going with the flow. And going with the flow ends in poop. Be a positive prophet because your words spoken negatively will also manifest. So, watch what is spoken by yourself and others over your life and especially your children. Words and images become reality. Life and death is in the power of spoken word.

By having a child while chasing my dreams, it added some pressure. I was working with my tent set up that summer and we were doing ok, but I knew the winter was coming. I was pricing food trucks and trailers and the price was out of my league. By now, my corporate credit was bad. I had to get a trailer in order to work year-round and be able to provide for my family. While working at Cowtown that summer, my brother-in-law spotted a trailer that an older man was working on and he prophesied and said, "That's your trailer." I remember going over to help the man pick up his generator with my brother, Russ. Remember, I said to have those who believe and want the best for you around so they only speak positively over your life. We made small talk and exchanged numbers. I actually thought nothing of it and kept trying to figure out how I would get a trailer for winter.

A couple of months passed and I ran into someone who told me I could actually sell and make big money at the Port of Wilmington, but I would need to have a trailer or a truck to come. I told myself I would be able to get there as soon as I got one. Shortly after, I got a call from the older man asking me if I wanted to buy his trailer. The only thing was that I didn't have any money. I told him yes, so he invited me to his house in Williamstown, NJ, to discuss things. I decided to bring Tonya and my eight-month-old, Azalea, with me, hoping it would cause the old rich man to have sympathy for this hard-working dreamer.

I say rich because the man had a farm with llamas and all types of animals. He had done well for himself and I was secretly hoping he would just give it to me, but I already knew nothing is given in this world. He wanted $20,000 for it and I had about $500 to my name. I told him I could make payments for a year and pay it off at the end of the year because, as soon as I got the truck, I was going to start making a lot of money at the port of Wilmington. He asked me if I had any money to put down, and I told him I only had about $500. He really wanted to sell it straight. After a while, he said he could not do it because he thought

I had money the way he saw me hustle. I remember feeling an overwhelming desire to obtain a trailer after he said no. I shook his hand, put my family in the car, and drove off. I felt so determined, I had an image in my mind while I was driving, thinking about how I was going to make it happen. I believe in myself. Just 25 minutes later, while driving home, I received a phone call and it was him, stating he had a change of heart. He agreed to work out a plan for me. I pulled over and just began to cry. I had known without a shadow of a doubt I was going to get a trailer, and that desire, that energy, that emotion caused the man to change his mind. I was excited. My brother's prophecy came true.

So, the old man set me up a plan to pay close to $700 a month. It was closer to $500 before he allowed his neighbor to influence him to charge more. I would have to pay a $20,000 last payment if I was going to own the trailer. I signed an "as is" contract. Within a month's time, most of the equipment no longer worked and I had to make do with what I had. I felt like I was taken advantage of but I thought I would soon make a lot of money and get it fixed. I felt it would be so easy. After getting a TWIC card, Delaware license, and permit, we got the job at the Port of Wilmington but things didn't go as planned. I thought I would make $1,000 a day at least, but I was making minimal money and still had to pay my brother.

I was just getting by but made sure I met the older man every month to make my payment on time and to talk about life for a little bit in his truck. The struggle was real and I didn't make enough money monthly to pay my mortgage or my house taxes. POOP JUICE.

I made a decision that I had to keep the trailer because that was how I made money, and if I tried to keep the house, there would be no way to make money if I lost the trailer. I was willing to sacrifice it in order to be able to continue my path to figure out how to make this million.

By the end of the year, I had accumulated only $5,000. It was two weeks away from my last payment, which was $20,000. For some reason, the older man called me and asked if I would have the money and seemed worried. I told him boldly YES in faith. The pressure was on and I had to lose all pride and focus on a solution. Nothing is impossible but I was not selling $15,000 worth of Zoagies in two weeks. So, I literally reached out to everyone I knew. People I believed had it. Call after call I was rejected. I told all of them I would give them 20% back if they loaned it to me. Their money would do better than any bank and I was looking to pay back in full within a year. Day after day, I called and waited for return calls—nothing. I would lend people money all the time when I was up but now I could not get any help. A week went by and I was still confident I was going to get $15,000. Remember, I said if we meditate a lot of times, the answers come to you. So, I settled down and I remembered two years ago, while in my backyard, my friend, Chill Will, said he would invest in me when he got his lawsuit money. So, I called him and asked if he ever got paid and he said yes and he was blowing it. I said immediately, give me $15,000 and I will give you $20,000 back in a year, and if I'm late, I will pay a $100 penalty every month until paid in full. To my delight, he agreed. Wow, I was putting in mad time calling everyone and asking for help, when if I would have just settled down, meditated, and listened to the voice within and acted on it, I would have avoided all that and got the money effortlessly.

Sometimes hard work is POOP JUICE, but a lot of times it's required. I SPOKE IN FAITH THAT I WOULD HAVE THE MONEY AND GOT IT WITH DAYS TO SPARE.

The high of achievement was short-lived. I got a knock on my door, and to my surprise, it was the state police. The officer asked if I was Ezell Barnes, and I said yes. Then he asked if I knew the old man and I said yes. The next statement broke my heart into pieces. "The older man said you stole his trailer and that he has been calling you with no answer. Is this your phone number?" the officer asked. I said, "Zell No! I have talked to this man every month for a year, and all of a sudden, he is senile." I was hurt but furious. The officer said it's a civil matter but to give the older man a call. I did it on the spot. I said to the man, "You sent the cops to my house?" And his response was, "Man, I don't know you," again, a crushing statement. I said, "I have known you and looked up to you and you did the worst thing possible by calling the cops on me, and acted like you don't know my number." The energy he spoke to me with was enough for me to slap an old man and really go in, but I held my composure at the same time, trying to comprehend what just happened. I came to find out he called all the places I did vending and told them I stole his trailer. How would that even be possible when you have all my information? How could you even feel this way when I've never even been late one time and the trailer is at my house zveryday? Nobody in their right mind would now give the money to this man after the humiliation and the willful attempt at tarnishing my business relationships.

To achieve our dreams and goals, tough decisions will have to be made, and I was faced with keeping my pride and not buying the trailer to prove a point to this man who didn't even apologize for his actions at the time, or have a lapse in business while I search for a $20,000 trailer, which may take some time. I really couldn't afford to stop business. I needed to get every penny to survive, especially with another winter approaching. I chose to purchase it and asked the old man a favor. I asked if he could do an insurance claim and get the trailer fixed because everything was broken within the first weeks of use. You would think that's the least he could do. He said, "Nope, your contract said 'as is'." I could not believe I was going to pay a total of $28,000 with the year payments included for a piece of junk. I really had to keep working, so I handed over the money and left feeling strange and abused but also determined that I would make things happen anyway, and I did. I got my trailer but it seemed like a cursed blessing if that's possible

CHAPTER 22

RELENTLESS PURSUIT

In order to make money vending, you have to literally go and pursue opportunities everywhere, almost every day, to try to get someone to allow you to participate in their event or to set up on a property. I searched daily for places to go. I went to the Sunoco in Pennsville a number of times and they always said, "No, we don't need that," and I would pop up here and there and ask to see if things changed. I remember asking Hanks in Salem if I could open up in their kitchen and they told me they didn't need drugs there, assuming that I would bring that to his store. I parked my trailer outside my house and would just be open in my hometown. Mostly that winter, I would send text blasts and hope that people would come in, but very few did. It got to the point where people asked me to stop texting them. The whole city knew I was there. I once drove around to try to get orders, and some guys on the corner told me that they were off that and that Zoagies was a fad and they were back eating and supporting the Chinese store. Boy was I boiling inside, and it zefinitely was slow, but I was still optimistic that I was gonna find my way. The winter is always tough, not only because sales are way down, but also because my home didn't have a heating system. When I was making money in Rainbow, I remodeled the house, but before completing it, I made a decision to start Zoagies. With the money needed to get the business going, I had nothing left over to finish the project, so I had a child and a wife in a home that had no heat. We just plugged up electric heaters and would stay in the bedroom. The winter bill was crazy. And the mortgage was not getting paid. It was hard to focus when every time you walked in the home, you saw bills. I made a decision to tell Tonya not to show me any more bills. I told myself I had to focus only on figuring out this Zoagie business. After a while, T showed me a piece of mail that was mind-blowing. It was a letter from our mortgage company saying they were forgiving the debt. We had to read it a number of times to believe it, but yes, the debt was gone. Now we were just responsible for taxes, which were also not getting paid and behind. I guess the house wasn't worth trying to foreclose on. We laugh and think about how all I had to do was turn my back on the bills and they disappear. I don't recommend doing that. It definitely was like one of those old-school testimonies you hear at church. In spring 2015, while out trying to find places to go, I was approached by a fellow vendor. I was told I needed to get downtown in Wilmington to their Wednesday farmer's market. He said there was a guy down there making $2,000 in three hours. That's all I needed to hear. So, the next Wednesday, I went down there and asked for who was in charge of the event and I was led to a guy that I call Caesar. I asked Caesar what I needed to do to be able to bring my trailer set up and be there the next week, and he said, "We are booked for years out," and turned his back to me. I watched all the people that were there and I saw the guy he spoke of doing great numbers. If I could make that type of money on a Wednesday, it would be a great help. The following week, I came back and asked Caesar again, "Do you think I could fit in that space over there?" Caesar said, "Didn't I tell you we're booked?" I said, "It looks like I can fit right there," with a smile and he ignored me. The following week, I arrived and asked again, "Hey, Caesar, I really believe I could fit there... right over there." This time, he kinda got angry with me and basically dismissed me. Meanwhile, while at the restaurant depot where all vendors meet to get their products, I ran into a lot of people that talked about the market and a lot of them said it is impossible to get down there if they already got who they want. I also heard things like they're racist and there's no way people of darker hue were getting down there. I heard everything but I had been down there trying to get there for three weeks straight and I was determined I was not going to let those POOP JUICE excuses stop me from helping my situation. The following week, I arrived at the farmer's market, and again, I said,

"Hey, Caesar, I really believe I could be an asset. There is nothing like Zoagies and I can fit right there." He looked at me in my eyes and said, "Man, you are zucking tenacious. Stop by next week and I'll get you a spot." Oh my Zod, I walked away beating my chest with tears in my eyes knowing I just did what others told me was impossible because I never told myself that. Persistent pursuit of your purpose is one of your powers. I'm always optimistic, so when the next week came, I went there, got set up, and was prepared in my mind to try to sell to 200 customers. We only served about 45. Caesar said, "You will be alright, just keep doing what you do." So, that year, we averaged around 50 orders. The next year, 80, the third year, we hit 100, and by the fourth year, we were doing the $2000 in business that drew me there in the first place. Caesar enjoyed watching the growth and was zappy. He gave me the opportunity. We are now good friends.

CHAPTER 23

BURNING DESIRE

In 2016, I decided to buy a smoker and start ZQ. This was my smoking business, and soon afterwards, many people were attracted to the smoke. One day while getting gas, I was approached by the owner of the gas station. He wanted to know if I would be willing to bring my smoker and sell food. This gas station was in the center of a busy truck stop. The owner said that $2,000-$5,000 a day could be expected. Hundreds of truckers pull in every day. I got excited and said, "This is what I've been working for." The guy said, "We can go 50/50." I told him that was too much but I could do it at a set price. He was very anxious and called me every day to see if I was coming. I told him I had to get permits first but he seemed pressed.

By the time I got my permit and showed up, he was gone. The guys there told me he was a scammer and not the owner. I was livid. My heart was set on getting into a high-traffic area and finally getting consistent money year-round. I was so angry and my emotions were running wild. I really wanted to get in a place where I could make money consistently, I just had to get the right opportunity, so I went down the street and asked a car dealer if I could pull up on his spot and do business so I could serve the truckers in the area. It was drawn out but, eventually, the answer came back no. I still just felt I had to have it so I went back to Sunoco in Pennsville, New Jersey, which was across from a Walmart.

I had asked them for four years if I could come and ask again, and I guess this time, my burning desire was at its highest and I could taste zuccess. I had little money and told them I would give them $300 to park and would not sell drinks or snacks but send them to their store. This would be month to month and I also told them after three to four months, we could renegotiate. They said yes after saying no so many times before. During that time, a couple of days a week, I would go and set up in Delaware outside a bar called Bobbi Rhians! My brother, Chef Mack, would do the cooking and I acted as a waiter, going inside, taking and delivering orders in a suit and chef hat. Many people thought I was crazy because of all the shootings in Wilmington that were happening, but I was there with my brother serving with a smile. I started late night in my own hood and did business until the am in Wilmington with no fear. I loved serving my product and they felt that and never had any problems.

I was excited to be on the busiest corner in Salem County, at Hook Road, and 49. I started doing promotions on social media and paid for my first ads on Facebook. This caused the whole county to see me, including a news writer who was dating one of my old basketball friends. She asked about me and he told her who I was and what I do, and she came and did a story. It was January 2017 and Zoagies was now front-page news. I changed the name of Sunoco to

Zunoco and people started pouring in. Finally, what I saw five years earlier was starting to happen. I had that faulty equipment and, all of a sudden, I had to use it to start serving 100-plus people every day, and then I got a call from Shannon, a legendary news reporter from ABC News. She asked to do an interview and, of course, I said yes. After the interview aired, Oh My Zod, pandemonium, the ZUNOCO was packed. I was not prepared for such crowds and immediately made enough money to buy some new fryers to help speed things up. I talked to and entertained zveryone.

No one had done anything like this before, and more and more people traveled to Zoagies and patiently waited hours for their food in the cold. I called them Zoagie Zombies. A week later, I got a call from Fox 29 Good Day Philadelphia, they asked for me to appear on the show live. Mike Jerrick and I had a ball and I shared some Zoagie dishes live in front of millions of people. The show was entertaining and drew more people to Zoagies.

Wow, my dream is here and we are operating at a million-dollar pace at this point. I then got a call from Fox 5 Chasing News and had an entertaining interview, bringing more attention.

Then I did the weekend Philler show on PHL-17. Soon after, I had an agent give me a call to do a Facetime interview for a Food Network show. I knocked it out of the park. Wow, I was going to be a star and Zoagies was trending. People from as far as four hours away were routinely pulling up to meet me and enjoy my creations. I was walking in my purpose, living in my prophecy, finally making money. I was able to pay off Chill Will and another loan I got from IBN for my smoker. I did all this in a predominantly white town and was serving all races the same love that drives me every day. They'd never had a vendor in Pennsville make such noise. A lot of Pennsville residents were getting the Zoagie zxperience for the first time and loved it.

CHAPTER 24

OVERCOME OBSTACLES/HATE

What a feeling of achievement! I had worked tirelessly for five years, and finally, things were looking up. I was employing around seven people at the time, just to try and keep up with the demand. A lot of money was coming in, but at the same time, a lot was going out. The craziest thing is, at this time, the highest thing on my menu was around $10, so no matter how many people I served, it wasn't that much in profits, but still better than the nothing I made over the previous five years.

Being on TV exposed me to the IRS. They came to the truck and saw my little money box, pad and paper, and said, "That has to change immediately." After seeing me on the news, they thought I was making big money and went back some years where I didn't file. I told them I didn't have any money and what they saw was just happening because of the new publicity. I got hooked up with a brilliant accountant right in Pennsville and got everything filed and put on a payment plan. Wow, money had to go out as soon as I started making it. The Zunoco owners were making more money than they ever had due to the crowds I was drawing but got greedy and came to me asking for more money, knowing that we had agreed to renegotiate in three to four months. They wanted over a 300% increase. I had to keep business going, so we settled for a more than 200% increase. This was not the first or last time I was taken advantage of.

Although I had lines, my profit margin was minimal, and as business owners, they knew that, but they couldn't stand to see me make money. A lot of people—and even in this case, partners—don't want to see you doing better than them and really hate on you in subtle ways. I owed people, so I paid off debts quickly thinking I would continue to grow from this point. Unbeknownst to me, I had people really hating me in the shadows. All I did was put smiles on faces and give unique tastes to all I met. I saw what looked like a white biker crew come to the truck one day, and as I always do, I greeted them with good energy and a smile, to only receive in return hard looks and snarls.

There are people who cannot stand to hear good things about others or about products. They will automatically go the opposite way just to be different or to show they don't go with the flow. This type of reaction is POOP JUICE! If you ever find yourself around those that just hate on things just because others like them, remove yourself from their presence because if you start to pop, they will try to undermine you immediately. These guys were loud and the leader looked at my zenu and said, "Give me the Po Boy," sarcastically, knowing what we have are

Zoagies. I record most interactions with permission, and when I asked this guy if I could record, he said he don't give a zuck but used the f. I said, "Sir, we love everyone here at Zoagies, why would you read our zenu then ask for a Po Boy, which is not listed?" His friends screamed out, "Because he is a zuckin zasshole," without the z, of course. I said, "It's cool, would you like a Zhrimp Zoagie?" He again said, "Yeah, the Po Boy." I said, "Much love," and served him. All this interaction was recorded. A week later, something surreal happened. My trailer was hit by a drive-by shooter. They were aiming at my brother in line. Just missing his head by inches. He heard the buzz pass his head. The criminals then went to my hometown and shot two brothers. One in the arm and one in the back, who both had to be hospitalized. They used a high-powered hunting gun that used metal shells other than bullets. I am still grateful they missed my brother-in-law at my location because that headshot would have been deadly. It would have also ended my business for sure.

I must admit, when I received the initial phone call from my brother, I was thinking selfishly. I asked if he called the cops, hoping he didn't because I knew my dream and all my hard work was about to be shattered, but I understood and it was necessary. He almost died. I said this will now be a part of my story. I really believe they wanted to shut down my business and to run me out of town. This all happened on Valentine's Day. The day of love, I was met with the ultimate hate. No greater hate can you receive than someone endangering your life and livelihood. I had only experienced what a million-dollar business would feel like for a month and a half before this surreal event.

The rumors began immediately, especially with all the cops surrounding my business. They said I was a drug dealer and this was my cover. I also got calls saying that I personally was shot, and people were upset. So, I made a video to let them know I was cool. I actually tried to downplay the ordeal because I knew people would be hesitant to come to Zoagies after this. I remember telling the shooters they will be caught because these officers don't eat donuts but eat Zoagies. That night, I made the decision that I was going to open the next day and told Tonya when the news came that I was not feeding into the negative and fear-mongering narrative. I was going to give them nothing but love and messages of overcoming crazy obstacles that come in life unexpectedly.

Fox 29 was the first to call and wanted me to come on live to discuss the tragedy. They asked questions such as, "Who do you know who would do this?" I never crossed a person in my life. Almost like, "What did you do to have this happen?" They said, "It has to be scary knowing your family is on that truck and you have people you don't know trying to harm you." I changed the narrative to how love conquers fear. If I would become fearful, my dreams would be over. I could have played victim and cried about how my daughter could have been hit, how my brother-in-law could have died, and my staff inside are traumatized, which would have been true. I could have complained about how I worked too hard for one shot from some haters to try to kill my dream. I could have chased sympathy from the viewers, but none of those things were going to help.

I always knew my purpose was to inspire and help people do more and become more and even to help others fulfill their dreams. This would be an opportunity in real-time to show how to have the excellent mindset of victor rather than victim. I am always aware of my story. I also believe that if you accept what happens to you as part of the process, you will learn from it as a necessary evil rather than have the 'woe is me' attitude, which is POOP JUICE! The ancient scriptures say that all things work for the good of them who believe. So, that means even what seems wrong and crazy is a part of your process. You overcome your obstacles by having a positive perception about them and push through and learn the necessary lessons. I had a yes attitude and chose to pursue my dream in love of its fulfillment.

The shooting was another moment in time that I had to choose to keep the vow I made to myself at 13, after I told my coach no when he asked me to get in a dangerous game. I vowed I would never back down or allow fear to cause me to hesitate again. A lot of people told me to quit because it was not worth it. I am not POOP JUICE, so I told them we were open at 11 am that day live on camera, not even 18 hours after being shot at. I didn't have a clue who did it. All I knew was that I sow love every day and was not supposed to reap hate. The news reporter said, "Wow, that's some faith. I would be scared, but feel like saying amen." I looked at the camera and said to all who were viewing, "Yes, I am open, and if you want to get a little faith, get some confidence, get some love, and become fearless, come to Zoagies because if you eat what I created, you might get a little of the creator in you."

I was showing the world that although I was met with hate and now had the obstacle of overcoming it, I was willing to stay in the game. We opened and very few people showed up in comparison to the day before. I knew people were afraid and I understood. It didn't help that rumors were around that I sold drugs and was using Zoagies as a cover. They said, "No one gets shot at for no reason." All these lies were like a plague. Everywhere I went, people asked if they were still shooting at me. I did not like the fact that I went from the guy who was on a million-dollar pace, who put smiles on everyone's face, who created the fried hoagie and Znglish to the guy who got shot at.

More news shows reported on the incident, even adding that the shooter used armor-piercing bullets to add to the fear. One channel was interviewing me and just cut because I wouldn't go with the fear-mongering. I just talked about Zoagies and spoke positively; they didn't like that. One news station seemed to have fun asking about rival food trucks that might want me gone but it all played a part in scaring the people away. I opened zveryday. I was getting little support but I had to pay everyone. I made sure they all got paid but I struggled.

CHAPTER 25

STAY FOCUSED ON THE END

After a few months passed, the Salem police solved the shooting crime. It was the rude white guys who visited my truck once. People came from everywhere like, "You suffered a hate crime," which is possible being all their targets were black men they didn't know. I don't know what they were thinking or what the motive of the two grown men would be to shoot people, but I am not trying to figure it out.

I was told I could sue the state for being a hate crime victim, which greatly affected my business. Before the shooting, we were on a million-plus-dollar pace, but now only doing pennies because of them. I know many influential people who could make this a big deal. Black man in white town gets business fired upon only because he is black and seems successful. I wanted no part of that. I would not be known as the guy who got his break because of a hate crime pay-off. I wanted my story to say, "He made it in spite of..." I would talk about it after I made it. So, I kept my focus on trying to get my customers back and bringing in new customers. These guys should thank me because I didn't even sign a complaint or pursue them. That's love of my enemy and myself, plus I couldn't afford to take my attention off keeping Zoagies alive. The guys were sentenced—one to probation and the other to five years, but he didn't even do a year in prison because of personal relationships with the DA. I know if I had done the same thing, I would have gotten at least 20 years. But I digress. There are many double standards in the world, but if you focus on them, you won't stay on the path to fulfilling your vision. I make no excuses, I don't focus on racism, I don't focus on double standards. They are what they are but will not keep me from achieving what I set out to do. Who cares that you have to work harder, so what, get it done! So what, there is discrimination, get it done! So what about your gender! Get it done. So what if you've been abused in any way as a child or adult! Get it done. Why let your life pass you by because someone did you wrong or your unfortunate circumstances? You can use the very thing to help propel you into purpose. Have you ever heard of turning your pain into gain? Please know you have the power to use what caused you to be a victim to be victorious.

Focusing on being victorious and not a victim will lead to an excellent existence in spite of your situations. I say, after you make your dreams happen, then if you like, you can turn your focus to fight against injustices. You can do this to make it easier for the next generation, but never let your focus be on obstacles, always focus on the fulfillment of your goals and let that lead you through your difficult times. Nothing is impossible for you to do with the right mindset and focus. A solution mindset is able to overcome most problems. Change your focus and you will change your destination. Regardless of how rough your road is, if you can stay focused on what it feels and looks like when you reach the end, you will eventually win.

CHAPTER 26

EVERY IDEA DOESN'T WORK

Within a couple of months, my customer base dwindled from hundreds a day to 15 to 20 orders. I got an offer, which was a few hundred dollars cheaper than Sunoco, to rent an open lot across the street that would provide more parking. It was the Fraternal Order of Police lot. People thought I went there for protection, but I needed every penny saved and rent was cheaper. Plus, Sunoco didn't deserve my money after taking advantage like they did. I thought this move would help, but I didn't notice any increase in business, so I did some offers and giveaways. They didn't help because all the freebie-takers would come, but no paying customers, and I would not make a dime some days. When things don't work, you must keep trying but switch things up. I got an offer to go in the middle of town in Pennsville at another gas station. I wasn't doing anything and it was actually free, so I gave it a shot. Would you believe that I could be out there 12 hours and wouldn't have five customers stop by? They all knew I was there. I felt they must have had a community conversation to not support me because how am I so loved but get no support? I guess I shot the gun. It got ugly when, one day, only one customer showed up. I was convinced they didn't want me there.

I went back to the FOP and had an idea for Zoagie Land. I built a 30×30 tent with the help of my neighbors across the street. They were so helpful. My Silverback friend and wife looked out. My sister, Gail, helped decorate it. I connected it to the trailer with three other tents. Used all my money to buy furniture and started promoting the family picnic atmosphere. Things did not change much. I had music and comedy nights but was left alone. One night, I did a whole comedy act by myself as if it was a packed house. I had a biker event that went well but the season was changing fast and I was running out of ideas for Zoagie Land. I put volleyball courts up, had horseshoes and many other games, but the struggle was real.

Once you taste what it is like to be busy, that becomes the standard. I was feeling like a one-hit wonder, but immediately flipped that and said, "I won't be a one-hit wonder."

CHAPTER 27

INFLUENCE

One thing is for certain—I have influence and a reputation that I have built over a lifetime. I make sure that if you're in my presence, you will feel important. Even if you're watching from afar, you will see my passion and work ethic.

While doing business in Pennsville, I met a lot of people, some on the chamber of commerce and other boards. They loved the energy I brought to the town when I first got there. I took no days off. Eventually, one person I made an impact on told another that they would be willing to invest in Zoagies if given a chance. I had offers to partner and invest since the backyard, but I was not willing to give up ownership.

During this time, I was struggling and my personal life was under stress. I couldn't pay the taxes on the house and they sold it in a tax sale. I was given 60 days to pay off the loan of $18,000 or I would be homeless. I called this guy I know, who I refer to as Captain Caveman. I asked him if he would be coming to Zoagies because I was told he was a willing investor. I told him that I needed help and that if he loaned me $12,000, I would give him $14,400 back in a year—20% flat is what I offered, which is great interest for a short term. He asked what it was for and I told him it was to save my home. He asked if I was sure that I could pay it back. I said with confidence that I would pay him back because Zoagie Land should do well. He looked at me and said, "I believe in you, chef," and shook my hand and gave me a check for $12,000. I don't know him and he only knows me by how I made him feel and how he sees me working crazy hours seven days a week. I was able to save my house only because my grind was so crazy. This gentleman felt led to invest in me. Some of you have to work on your reputation in order to have influence. A lot of entrepreneurs start out looking for support, but your reputation is one of laziness or one of incompleteness. You never finish what you start, you complain all the time, have beef with people and even share it on social media, have not been trustworthy in the past, burned bridges, and never applied yourself to anything long enough to become excellent at it. This is POOP JUICE and your expectation of support is a bad case of entitlement. A good name is worth more than treasure, the scripture says, and you must guard your reputation with your life. Your name is built over time, and the younger you start, the better, but starting today is a great choice too. Consistently operating under excellent principles and working hard will give you a reputable name in time. My name and reputation got me two unsecured loans and a lease-to-own deal from one guy who grew up with me, another who knew of me for five months, and the old man who just saw me working one day and had a brief interaction with me. Your influence and your name can also help you to network with those who can put you in position and shortcut your path to excellence.

CHAPTER 28

NEVER GIVE UP

Zoagie Land flopped and I could not believe that after the shooting incident, Salem County as a whole wrote me off. That setup was really nice but was so slow, one employee, Chef Mack, ran the no-show. But not only Salem County, but the Food Network deal went away and also a deal for the Walmart parking lot. I made my last payment at the FOP and basically went out of business, but I was not closing or giving up.

I licked my wounds and went back to my home in Salem. I tried to get a welcome back reception but was met with minimum support. My mind was racing at all times, searching for a solution. My family and friends said, "Just get a job or sell Rainbows again." I could not listen to them. I had tasted what it felt like to be successful, and knew that whatever I could do once, I could do again. I just had to remember the success process.

I opened zveryday on the side of my house. How humbling to be right back where you started. I was putting in long hours making videos and driving around town to create some business. I had to make payments on that $12,000 loan. I would have some days that were just awful. On two different occasions, I made just $37, which didn't even cover the propane. I remember coming in the house all the time to see Azalea and T upstairs keeping busy. They started a show, "In our mind is just fine." They pretended to travel the world and adapt the customs of different people. I was like, I am taking so long to make this dream happen that they just decided to go there in their minds. Well, that is not fine with me. I wrote and said we would do that in real-time. So, I continued to work and think. I did imagine the stress she was under trying to be supportive with a child. I would hear Tonya listening to recordings about how dollars want us all the time. Even the baby was meditating.

CHAPTER 29

NEVER GET LOCKED IN

While working on the side of my house one night, a bar owner asked if I would come and work the kitchen. The bar was called The People's Tavern. He told me he would get a contract together if I was interested. I was interested, but I knew that the bar must have needed a spark and he wanted Zoagies to be that. I wrote up my own contract, making it a month-to-month deal and we both could terminate at any time if it was not mutually beneficial going forward. I ran into a lot of business owners who were shrewd. They would lock you into a contract, and if things were not working out, they would press you even if it was only beneficial to them. Even get the law involved. I enjoy my freedom and will not willingly give my power over to another for an extended period of time, especially while dream chasing. Opportunities will always come, and some are better than others. I gave him the contract and he said he would have his lawyers look at it and then we could start. Month-to-month is an excellent way of doing business while trying to find your way.

Zoagies now had an indoor location. The building was nice and I thought I would do well. We started off with a bang. Local businesses were overwhelming me with lunch orders. I actually couldn't keep up with myself, so I hired a person to help. The bar life was crazy. I never hung out, but now it was like I was out every night. Days started at 9 am, would open at 11 am, and close at midnight during the week and after 2 am on the weekends.

I started at the end of December and had a grand opening on January 1st. I met a lot of people and would get a monthly visit from Captain Caveman. He would order and collect his money at the same time. I had a ball for most of the time I was there. But after a few fights and a state police incident, things started slowing down. I like having the covering and storage of the building, but I still was searching for that thing that would have me back in the limelight and on my way to millions.

I was thankful that I didn't sign a long-term lease because, by the summer, things fell off so much, the owner offered to sell me the spot. The spot's reputation had been damaged and nothing I could do was going to change it.

CHAPTER 30

KEEP SEARCHING

Every opportunity I have, I am very optimistic. I always think this is the one, and it's going to get me out of poverty and get me to a place I can be proud of.

Coming from the hood, I initially set my prices really low. And I must admit, I had trepidation about raising them. I had an opportunity to serve at the Nuclear Power Plant and I knew I had to change my prices beforehand. I had a talk with a friend and he said I should go up 50 cents to a dollar. I chose to raise it almost 100% from $8 to $15 with fries. To my surprise, most people knew about Zoagies and just never tried it. They paid without a problem. A lot of them did remind me I was shot at. There was a lot of security there and they soon stopped the program. I got a call from Amazon soon after. Maybe this will be where I get out of poverty, I thought. I told them I needed to make $1,000 a day and I had staff to get paid. They said it should be no problem. I was scheduled for twice a day 10 am-2 pm and 8 pm-10 pm. It was very inconvenient, especially because I mostly sold $5 and $10 No Dough platters to people who only had 30 min breaks. We got a lot of exposure but the numbers dwindled as the shopping season was over and their seasonal staff was let go. I asked if they could cover what I didn't make so it could be worth my time. They declined and said to give it time. Well, I had no time, I needed money right away. I was threatened that if I didn't show anyway, even though I wasn't making any money, that they would make sure I wouldn't sell at any Amazon anywhere. Since they had no concern for my struggle, I moved on to UPS.

UPS was surrounded by many other warehouses and we were doing well until they said I could no longer be on the street because they were doing construction down the street. Seemed like zverywhere I went was promising but ended the same way. I didn't understand considering that all I heard were great things about my business, but I continued my search for a place where the honeymoon would last. No matter what you have going on, you must tell yourself this is a part of the process and keep swinging. The answer is going to be found only by those who don't stop searching for it. Again, your persistent pursuit of your goal is your way to excellence.

CHAPTER 31

NOTHING IS GUARANTEED

One of my original goals was to be zuccessful in my hometown. Of course, I had been there a number of times over the years. The busiest spot in Salem is East Side Sunoco. I used to sit there and watch how many people went there a day and thought I would do well. One thing that was different since being on the news was that it was not as hard to get a chance to set up. I talked to the owner and he agreed that I could use his place free of charge, I just could not sell drinks and snacks. No problem. After waiting months for my permit in town, I started working long hours and was doing ok. Not the numbers I thought I would do, but I was in my hometown and not at my house. The only drawback was that Salem does not allow you to vend on Sundays, which is typically a big day for Zoagies. So, on Sundays, I worked somewhere else. No days off is my motto.

Most Sundays I would go to Penns Grove and do business, and one Sunday, we booked an event in Philly at Penn's Landing. The Africana Fest! This was life-changing. We served 650 people in six hours doing No Doughs and earned a record at that time of more than $7,000. I figured out a system that could move crowds very quickly, and with another two people, we could almost double that number. I thought at this point, we should go where the masses of people are. I thought Atlanta, Georgia would be the place to go. So, we booked the Sweet Auburn Music Festival for the end of September 2019. We had some momentum going in Salem, but the time had come for us to drive to Atlanta. I had a 2000 Ford 250 that was in ok shape, so I got it serviced and bought new tires for the trailer. I told everyone that I was going to shake up the city and be on the radio when I got there. I also felt there was a high percentage of successful people and celebrities in the city, which could lead to great networking. I am zifferent. I would have to stand out.

My team was seven deep, including Tonya and Azalea. It took 20 hours to get there and I hit a curve on my first turn in the city and blew the brand-new tire. We limped into the festival in the morning, only to find out our trailer was too big for the spot assigned. Oh my Zod, I have traveled 20 hours for this. I spent most of my money on product, hoping to flip it like I did at Africana Fest, and I couldn't even get in my spot. They told me I would be able to set up out front and I thought maybe this would be better. While I was waiting, my truck lost its brakes and started rolling backwards. I got it stopped and found that the brake line had broken. I dropped the trailer and parked it across the street. Thankfully, my mechanic was hard-headed and drove his truck too, even though I tried to get him to ride with me.

Of course, it was a heat wave in September with temperatures above 100 degrees. The event started and was slow. I noticed that most of the people were in the food area and were not accustomed to food out by the stage. I didn't plan on having to sell people on Zoagies, but I did. I had the team giving out samples. My slogan is, "Put it in their mouth and they're hooked no doubt!" Well, we had to do that all day and explain what a Zoagie was. This was not the thousand sales I envisioned.

I saw the radio station across the way and told the team I was going to give them a Zoagie and get on air. I went to the room to chill for an hour and the team jumped the gun. Told me they gave the station a Zoagie and they wanted to interview me. The brother asked if I wanted him to do it and I said, "ZELL NO! I will be right there."

When I arrived, there was a lady getting interviewed but didn't say much. Big Tigger asked me if I was ready and gave me earphones with a mic and said we were live. He made one statement about a guy from Jersey down here, then I took over. I screamed, "TWENTY ZUCKING HOURS!" and everyone turned around. I said, "I am Chef Zoagie, you all should know me and follow me on all social sites. Everyone here has the same thing, but I got ZISH, ZHRIMP,

ZHICKEN, AND ZRAB LIKE YOU NEVER HAD!!!" People started walking towards me and I kept freestyling. By the time I was done, Big Tigger asked me, "Who are you?" I told him, "I am the zelebrity the people haven't met yet." He said, "Zhit, you was ready." I replied, "I didn't drive 20 hours not to be ready." I actually said this would happen. I was talking to zveryone. The radio station even offered me an opportunity to cater for them if I decided to stay. I zefinetly had a thought to stay. My friends who live there were excited to see me there and also thought I should stay.

Things really picked up after my interview but not enough to do damage to all the supply. The next day, we got on another new station, this time, my daughter stole the show. I had her and Tonya out with me handing out samples. We did ok but nothing like I imagined.

CHAPTER 32

A TRUE HUSTLER

A lot of people talk about hustle but few truly do it. It is important as an entrepreneur to have a hustler spirit. This means you are ready and able to adapt to any surroundings and move your product or make connections. Always looking for opportunities to sell. The event was two days. I told the team I would pay for their flights back if they wanted because I was staying after we got the brake line and tire fixed. Everyone wanted to stay. So, I told them I was going to build the business from scratch in the ATL, plus I had to get rid of close to a thousand pounds of food. I saw a corner we passed when going to Autozone and set that as my target. I noticed at night there were vendors hustling with no problem around the college campus. I went downtown to see what was needed for licenses and permits and was not in a position to make it happen yet. So, I was willing to break the rules to get started.

We finally found a tire, fixed the brake line, and was ready to go. Unfortunately, we came back to a boot on the truck. Spent money on that, a new Airbnb, and went to the spot. It started off slow, but every red light we would run over and give out samples. Remember to put it in their mouth and they're hooked. People started calling others and telling them Jersey is down here. The lot was getting busy, then two guys pulled up. I hoped it was not their property but they came for food. After they ate, they asked if I wanted to come to Jonesboro. They were leaving town and would be back to discuss the deal. I told them that we didn't need to wait. I asked, "Do you think I will sell 100 customers a day?" They answered, "Yes." I let them know I wouldn't sell drinks and snacks so that money would be theirs. I said half of them would buy drinks, and at $2 apiece, that would be $100 a day, $3,000 a month, not including gas and other products. He said, "Deal." Look at that opportunity coming my way while I am on the grind. A little while later, a lady from the health department showed up and shut us down. I knew it was a possibility, but hoped to get a month in before I got caught. After that, we switched to hustling at night. I walked the streets and gave out samples and sold Zoagies in barber shops and outside of clubs. My friend connected me to one club called Parlor, and we served them and the clubs down the street. My team was seeing what hustle was all about.

We went to Jonesboro and started doing business. It seemed like everything I thought was going to pop, I wound up having to hustle up the business. We were doing good even though we were illegally operating. It all came to a halt when a teammate overfilled the generator with oil. I was risking losing all this fresh product if I did not get it sold, and now I couldn't work at night. I had just paid for a seven-day Airbnb but had to pack up and leave.

CHAPTER 33

YOU WIN OR YOU LEARN

I was very disappointed that I made the decision to go back home. But I knew that I could sell most of my product at Cheyney Homecoming. I was also proud that I went for it in foreign territory and really felt that if I had the funds and credit, Zoagies would be huge in ATL within a couple of months. I saw what was needed for licenses and made connections that would make my return triumphant. I zefinitely will be financially well and have great credit when I return.

It was a long 20-hour ride back. I really wanted my story to say, "He went and never came back until he was rich," but I learned a lot.

I only look at things that I do as lessons and stepping stones to blessings. Never do I see myself as a failure because things don't work out. I keep it moving, trusting that it is a part of my process to become excellent in whatever I am doing. We made it back in time for homecoming and sold most of the product because we stayed after other vendors were gone. I learned a long time ago, you don't have to be the best, you just have to have the most endurance. I can work many days in a row with no sleep if I have to. I would rather not, but I had to a couple of times. When I went back to Sunoco, all my momentum was gone and I learned that you never break momentum, you ride it out. If you're pursuing greatness, then it is worth it.

CHAPTER 34

APPLIED KNOWLEDGE IS WISDOM

Things were slow and I had a lot of time to think and read. A friend of mine gave me a book, "Million dollar Success Habits" by Dean Graziosi, and I read the whole thing. I immediately applied the things I learned. Paraphrasing: One thing was for me to sit back and visualize what my best year ever would look like and write it down. He then said, "What does it feel like in that place of accomplishment? How you feel then, I need you to hold on to it and keep it every day as you go to make it happen." I did this exercise and finally cleared my mind enough to come up with answers to get me there. During meditation, I was able to look back and see all that took place before business blew up the first time. There was a strategy that started it all and was abandoned soon after. Three years had passed. I was living with holes in my ceiling, holes in my floors, and all I had to do was INVEST IN MY MARKETING and CHANGE WHO I MARKET TO. I had learned that no matter how creative I was making videos and posting them on social media, those who knew me were not going to share it. So, year after year, I was beating a dead horse. I was very limited with my reach. As soon as I put some money behind my ads, I began to get views. I always knew I was a purple cow, but my county was too used to seeing me. I made a zrab and zhrimp video that got like 50,000 views and I only put a little money behind it. I advertised everywhere but Salem County, and people started showing up. My followers began to increase dramatically also. I really shook my head because I could have done this in year two and saved myself a lot of time. But I was zappy to find the answer to my problem.

CHAPTER 35

STAY CREATIVE

You are an asset to the world when you are yourself. Creativity is a gift you have because, if you are yourself, you're going to do things differently than anyone else. I was getting more and more buzz from around the tri-state area and my videos were being seen by thousands. For eight years prior, I was lucky to get a couple hundred. Man, I wish I knew this earlier, but I will help others avoid my headaches. I noticed a lot of people use popular posts to plug their own products. One person was really hating, saying that I was using imitation crab and fake shrimp and that I should be selling lobster rolls as he plugged his friends' business. I said I would check out the lobster next time I went to the depot. To my surprise, it was over $30 a pound. I saw that they sold tiny lobster rolls for $20- $28. This gave me the idea to create a Triple Zea MONSTER. I would combine the zhrimp, zrab, and zobster and lay it in a fried roll. I did a video and it did numbers. I priced it at $50. I learned the last time I was popular, I disrespected myself by pricing such a unique product so low. I once was told by my friend, Jul, that when I was on TV, the people came to see the speaker and I traded them an $8 sammich and walked out of my house. I wouldn't make that mistake again. I was not going to be a one-hit wonder.

A lot of people from my town saw the video and came to the truck but got upset with me because of the price. I said this was exclusive and not for everyone. They told me to my face that no one was going to spend $50 for a sandwich on a zuckin food truck. I waited until later that same day the video was posted to sell the first one to a local. I took a picture of the guy holding it and posted it. Then the second, the third, and it kept going. So much for them telling me what others were not going to do. I don't receive doomsday prophecies, I only receive what I speak over myself.

I later got a message from a company that wanted to know if they could add fish to the Triple Zea MONSTER. I said yes, and told them the price. I never heard from them but the ZOCHNESS MONSTER was born. ZISH, ZHRIMP, ZRAB, AND ZOBSTER all on a fried or grilled roll for $60. I made a video making it and got hundreds of thousands to view it. Hundreds of people were coming to Zoagies for the Monster but if they didn't have the money, they grabbed an $18 zrab and zhrimp. We began to draw famous foodies and got rave reviews. By May 2020, my videos reached over a million people during the pandemic.

CHAPTER 36

PANDEMIC PROOF

Before the pandemic hit, I was just getting my stride. Luckily, the state didn't shut down food trucks but only restricted restaurants. Zoagies was the hot spot. I was so proud, we were in my hometown and were on a 2-million-dollar pace. I did something never done before in my town by drawing hundreds daily from New York, North Jersey, Cumberland County, Delaware, Baltimore, Philadelphia, Chester, and DC. I was told it was impossible by my mentor to do numbers in an impoverished small town, but I was doing it right before their eyes.

The Sunoco owner was not cool with all the people coming to Zoagies. He started talking about bills and parking. He would, in the beginning, tell me my prices were too high and wouldn't work. I never tried to tell him how to run his business... but I digress. He lost his mind watching a crowd and they paid $50 and $60 apiece. Tension rose and we were running out of room, so after I got threatened, I picked up my business and went back to Pennsville to use the parking lot. I no longer depended on my home county. I now had the keys to grow without them. We had the parking lot packed immediately, and after two weeks, we got shut down in the middle of serving people. I filled out all the paperwork but it was some permit issues they wanted cleared up. I went to Penns Grove for the weekends and waited for my everyday permit in Pennsville. Penns Grove had cars lined up for miles. It was unlike anything they saw. Zoagies had consistent three and four-hour waits, and all this during a pandemic. I dropped my first $100 Zoagie on my birthday. It was called ZODZILLA. I advertised it ahead of time and people were lined up waiting. Everything you create will sell if you are sold on it first. Your energy is different when you really believe in something rather than just hoping it catches.

While waiting for permits, Zoagies had to close for a month because of exposure to the Coronavirus. This really killed our momentum. During our time off, I made a bad investment into another food truck. POOP JUICE! I say bad because I promised I would go new to not go through the same problems I had with the first. And this thing was full of problems. I tried to get new but I would have had to wait three months, so I ran out of patience because I wanted to serve customers faster. You have to stick to your promises.

CHAPTER 37

ALWAYS REACH UP

When we have momentum in life and are growing, we have a tendency to reach back prematurely to help others or link with those trying to catch a ride. I have always helped those around me. But when it came to me getting a new truck, I thought it was ok to add some friends to the project. They tried their best; they were just in over their heads when it came down to deadlines.

I purchased the truck in June 2020 and didn't get it in service until May 2021. I turned away hundreds of thousands of dollars because I didn't have my truck in service. When I started using the truck, the plumbing immediately blew and I had to get someone to fix it.

After driving the truck to Bridgeton, I felt the transmission going.

The reverse totally went and I still drove it every day to locations to serve because, in order to reach that million, I couldn't take any days off. I made a video about how you don't need to reverse, just go forward cautiously so you never have to look back. While driving 35 miles per hour max.

The first day the monster truck opened in Wilmington at the Rodney Square farmers market, the fire suppression blew and sprayed chemicals throughout the whole truck. It was over a thousand dollars of orders that had to be refunded. The people watched in awe. I thought I lost my whole investment in less than two hours. I got some professionals to clean it up and got it back in service the next week. The chemicals took all the shine away. I got a higher temp suppression put in place. All this would have been avoided if I got a brand-new truck. It was my fault, I allowed impatience to cause me to not do what I planned. Avoid putting your business in the hands of people you cannot sue. Make sure they are fully insured and have rave reviews. If I was dependent on that truck, I would have gone out of business before I started.

Because of my decision and other factors, Zoagies fell short of a million in 2020. Another factor was that I slowed down on my social media marketing because trying to keep crowds of people occupied for hours was exhausting. What a POOP JUICE decision. You never fall back on your marketing. It is better to deal with too much than to deal with not enough. The great thing is, after a short period of investing in your marketing, you can build back the momentum.

CHAPTER 38

THERE IS MORE THAN ONE WAY

People are always searching for a path that will lead to success. The problem is, there are many paths. It is very popular to hear about having multiple streams of income in order to become wealthy. This is true, but you usually need to master one stream in order to free yourself up to invest in others. By January 2021, I decided I was going to get into stocks and crypto. I was POOP JUICE and had no knowledge at all. I said to myself, I am about to become Warren Zuffet. After my proclamation, I went to the library and purchased a number of books on the subject of stocks.

Immediately, I began reading and applying things I learned. Some people buy books but don't read them, and some read them and don't apply what they learn, and that's POOP JUICE!

I searched and found a couple of YouTube stock analysts on the subjects to listen to. I woke up to hearing dialogue and tips and went to sleep hearing the same. I would go to Zoagies daily to make sure things were running right, then return to my study. Within three months of study, I had opened multiple investment accounts and was making more money than I did on the Zoagie truck with much less effort. I can't believe I didn't decide to invest in the markets sooner. I identified myself as a long-term investor and invested in things I felt had a great usage and would be in demand in the future. I also jumped into some plays that I should have grabbed and sold, but my nature to want the seeds to stay planted to get maximum return over time got the best of me. One of my many investments gave a return of $80,000 in less than three months. I had at one point 90% of 40-plus investments in the green. I grew over a $200,000 portfolio in less than a year. One thing for sure is that you have to have patience and understand how the market works in cycles and not ever invest what you can't afford to lose. As I write this, the market is way down and a lot of my investments are now dropping. One mindset is to pull your money so you won't lose it all, and the other is to let it drop. If they are good companies, when it bottoms, make sure to take advantage of the prices so when the tide turns, you can ride it to the promised land. I chose the second option and am looking to reap big in the future.

One thing I learned was that it is so much better to invest your money in ways that it works for you versus you working for it. I am a firm believer in working very hard to accomplish anything, but I admit it is 100% better for your money to work hard for you. Big difference in owning a business vs the business owning you. I am now just reaping the benefits of owning Zoagies vs working in Zoagies. I can earn money without showing up if I choose. That is liberating. But my money pays for it. How do you earn extra money to invest? One of the best things to do is make sure your credit score is good to excellent.

I had a very difficult time due to bad banking credit but survived because of great hood credit. My score was 560. I decided to study about the subject and repaired my own credit. I used a simple 609 letter, negotiated, and paid off some accounts and brought all accounts current. The biggest jump in my score came when I jumped on my sister's credit card as an authorized user and paid all my cards down to less than 5% usage. It took less than a year for my credit score to rise to 725, 745, and 808. When you have good credit, you are able to leverage it to create income streams for yourself. There are millions of people with POOP JUICE credit who will pay you just because you have good credit. Authorized user accounts are very lucrative if you promote and structure it right. It doesn't take a lot of effort to get paid for maintaining your credit. With credit or without, you can start a business. Usually, you start out as owners/operators, but hopefully, you will build it enough that you can pay others to run it for you. Find a product you believe in that people also want and sell it to them. Provide a service to others. Get a higher-paying job and live below your means. Earn a raise on the job or receive extra tips for providing excellent service or products. All these things can earn you extra money, and you can then find places to put it in order for it to increase over time. The goal of this passive income is to provide a lifestyle of freedom.

CHAPTER 39

DO MORE, BECOME MORE

Going the extra mile is one of the fastest ways to excellence. Somehow, during our youth, a lot of us got shamed for doing too much. We made a habit of doing just enough or less than required at most things. If you asked or answered too many questions in school, you were called the teacher's pet. If you played on a team and did anything extra, you were clowned. When we worked jobs and did extra, we were called zass kissers. All these shame tactics worked like a charm and kept people being POOP JUICE PERFORMERS.

Excellence is the opposite. When you go the extra mile, it immediately separates you from the pack and makes you more valuable. Many are searching for ways to increase income and all they have to do is increase their work habits. Do more than what you're paid for consistently and you will start to get paid more than you're working for. Promotions and pay raises are almost automatic when you become the worker who cannot be replaced. They say your gift will make room for you. Your habit of always doing more zefinitely will bring you into the big rooms.

At Zoagies, I always give more than what I am getting paid for. Actually, I wasn't getting paid at all for years, but I served the people and engaged the people like no other. I know the price of that is high but I give it for free, extra on top of them having a unique product. They get engagement, service, smiles, and entertainment. Going the extra mile has opened crazy doors and has caused Zoagies to continue to grow in popularity and in revenue. Work your way into better positions, better pay, and into a better life. Do extra with a smile and consistently sow extra energy into whatever you're doing, and you will rise to excellence in due time.

CHAPTER 40

MORE MONEY, MORE PROBLEMS

When dealing with any business that involves cash, you must be organized and daily balance your numbers. My mother, from the time I started Zoagies and having help, told me to watch my money because people steal. I always told her the millionaires I know don't worry about it. They monitor it so it won't be outrageous but they focus on creating more revenue.

Well, over the years, I had family and friends steal from me because it was easy to. I made some POOP JUICE decisions and responded to those willing to steal from me when I worked countless hours to make sure they had a paycheck. The worst decision was not firing them on the spot. A couple of times I got confrontational because of the gall of those who are close to me. I hired many ex-cons, ex-addicts, ex-drunks, and people hard on their luck, hoping to help change their lives.

Over the years, I have caught those close to me stealing, having to strip them out of their clothes just to find my money on them. Others had whole schemes passing money off to their people at events. I ran through cars in search for my money, and after all this, I never changed until September 2021. We normally were stationary but hit it big moving to Delaware in August 2021. It seemed like the whole state was coming out. People were lined up and we were setting records daily and had our largest month of $168,000 in August and had a huge September. My first eight years, I had a money box and didn't do well tracking daily totals. But in 2020, I became a clover member, and for two years, I have every transaction recorded. This enabled me to keep track of everything from cash received, credit, and daily inventory.

It was only after I consistently didn't have enough money, even though I deposited every dime, that I checked the cash received vs the cash deposited. I found that every month for those years, there were $3,000-$15,000 discrepancies, totaling over $100,000. Wow. I seriously had to ask Tonya if she was stashing. At this point, everyone was a suspect. There was so much money coming through that, unfortunately, a few of my highest-paid employees thought it was ok to take their own bonuses. I guess they were encouraged especially after taking money and I said nothing because I was POOP JUICE for not checking. I guess they were thinking I was stupid since they were getting away with it. My mom, sisters, and lastly, my guy I was renting the lot from blatantly told me they were taking my money and they were right. I tried to set a trap to catch the thief by checking the balance when they were off, but no matter who was off, it was still short. So, I let the team know together that I knew out of the 12 employees it was a team effort to steal money. I fired no one because I didn't have proof of who it was. I just put cameras up and made sure I did what I was supposed to do. I balanced the register every night, changed some protocol, and gave a clear description of activities that would cause immediate discharge. I slowly watched people fire themselves. After they knew that I KNEW, trust, the energy was different. No matter what, I still needed to serve the masses that were coming to Zoagies.

It put a toll on me knowing it was my fault. I was unprofessional about the accounting of the business. Yes, I could blame them, but I took full responsibility for setting the easy-going atmosphere that was all too tempting. One time, after they knew that I knew they were stealing, someone tried me again. The drawer was short. So, when it was time to give tip bonuses, I subtracted what the drawer was owed. You should have seen their faces. I learned instantly that most people don't care unless it affects their pockets. I NEVER had another problem.

I suffered great losses and learned tough lessons during the growth of Zoagies. I had friends turn on me. I had employees who made more money than they ever had try to sabotage me from within. I had people show disrespect for what I had built. I had rocks thrown at my truck while driving. I had my trailer shot up. I had blatant lies told about me. Even a disgruntled ex-employee that I put in position making great money even went to the health department in an attempt to destroy my business. I had my hometown businesses complain to the council. I was having to pay huge IRS back payments. All this because I want to be excellent and want to leave a legacy. When you are totally focused on getting to your end goal, you are willing to go through the trials and tribulations, and I have experienced a lot.

CHAPTER 41

FIGHTING FOR THE $1,000,000 FINISH

One thing is for sure... I hate a honeymoon that doesn't last. I will always give my all for the entirety of my relationships, but most cities I come to, they show love for a number of months then fall off. Bear Delaware was no different. Sadly, the majority of business I get usually travels 40 minutes and up to two hours to get to me. So, when fall hits, it seems we take a hit. Zoagies' pace fell from $168,000 in August to a yearly low of $60,000 in November. This was traumatizing. I was less than $100,000 away from my 10-year goal of $1,000,000 in a year. I could not handle the thought of being so close to missing it. A lot of those I talked to were like, "Man, $900,000 is amazing," but that was not the magical number of

$1,000,000 I was working towards. I knew from starting in a backyard to earning $1,000,000 in a year would be newsworthy and an excellent accomplishment. I had some brothers from a tire shop stop by and ask for me to bring my trailer to serve all the truck drivers. I told them I would have to get them put in my insurance plan. The guys said I didn't need it as they were the managers. I knew immediately this was a bad idea but my business was practically dead, so I risked it thinking maybe I could get a few good weeks in before I get shut down. So, I moved my business from Delaware back to Jersey. After one day, the buzz was building but I got a call in the morning that I had to leave immediately. Wow, these guys sold a dream acting like they had clout and didn't have anything but mouth. After announcing my departure two days before, I announced my return. I turned up my paid advertising and called some Philly and Delaware influencers to see if that would give me a push and it did. I thought I would probably make it, but with the holidays, I wasn't sure. The whole year, I had two trucks but used one for storage. I got the idea to send one to Bridgeton, New Jersey, the second week in December. This was a great idea.

All day every day, I thought about doing a million in a year. I was borderline stressing the last two months because of the massive drop in business, which, again, was my fault. My mind was not at ease. I had this book also on the back burner knowing I said it would be done long ago. But all things work together for the good indeed.

It is so much better to release this book after the fact that... on DECEMBER 17, 2021, ZOAGIES CROSSED A MILLION DOLLARS!!!!! WOOOOHOOOOO!!!!! MY DREAM FULFILLED!! IT WAS A SURREAL FEELING!!

I looked at those seven figures on my clover account and nodded my head yes and spoke to myself, "You made this happen, you are a true prophet. You are a beast. You did it with less! You made no excuses! You believed in yourself! You went through the storms! You took no days off! You learned lessons! You paid attention to what works! You loved in spite of hate! You forgave people and gave grace! You kept your eyes on the prize! You stayed creative! You stayed true to you! You invested in you! You will inspire millions! Your story will be told! You kept your foot on the gas and finished with Zoagies doing over $1,040,000 for the year of 2021!"

This was all done while living in an impoverished town. On a street that has over 20 abandoned and decaying homes, which I see daily when I leave the house. Our home is a legally uninhabitable home because it has no heating system with no kitchen cabinets, and a hole in the floor and ceiling that leaked when flushing the toilet. We will relocate soon. I mentioned this to prove it is not about where you are from, it is about where your mind is. My vision of a multi-million-dollar business was clear regardless of my circumstances and living situation. My family mastered the art of being comfortable with being uncomfortable while in pursuit of our goal. The sacrifices were great but the reward will be greater.

CHAPTER 42

NEW BEGINNINGS, NEW GOALS

Success always leaves clues. In achieving our goal of $1,000,000 in a year, we learned at the very end we could run two locations at the same time. We also learned that Zoagies are in crazy demand, and if we were to travel to new markets, it would always be pandemonium.

In January 2022, I immediately started looking for a new market in Jersey and a new city in Delaware to do business. By February the 1st, I had moved the monster truck to New Castle, Delaware to a spot I spoke of being at years before. And by March 1st, 2022, I started our second location in Mt. Laurel, New Jersey at Lakou Event space. By paying attention and implementing what I learned from the success in 2021, Zoagies is on pace to increase business by 50% in 2022 and can possibly hit $2,000,000 if we decide to move three or four times this year. I can see it just comes down to whether I want to do what it takes to make it happen. I also look to begin my speaking career with this book being my foundation. I am optimistic, I am excited, and I have a burning desire to inspire!

CHAPTER 43

ONE LAST STORY AND ADVICE

A couple of years back, I again experienced the great feeling of being excellent at what I do right after experiencing some disappointment. Over the years, I had become one of the top 1% basket makers in the world, but missed two free throws that led to my team being upset during a playoff game. I was determined to be better, so I went to the gym every day for those couple of months I was at my mom's until I was able to knock down 100 free throws in a row, shooting 100%. I was elated because I only know of a handful of people to have ever done that. Later, I got hurt and was unable to jump, but I loved playing so much that I created a whole new style of basket-making to be able to still perform. The new style made me even more productive in the game, although I could barely move. I recorded myself during basket-making practice. I would consistently shoot and make over 90% of my baskets, from three-point to mid-range. One recording, which I posted to YouTube, shows me making 209-230 baskets from all over the court. This prompted me to create a basket-making program that helped individuals increase their basket-making percentages by 20%-40%. I believe one day it will help countless thousands improve their game. Turn your pain into your gain.

I always believed that I could do anything and it contradicted everyone and everything around me. When I would watch a person do something miraculous, I would see everyone in amazement and watch them count the person as a god. They never had the thought that it was possible for them also. When I saw someone accomplish something amazing, I would immediately ask myself a very powerful, life-giving question. How can I do that? I found out that if I asked that question, it would force my brain to find ways and I was willing to do whatever it took to make it happen. Some people do have natural gifts, and others have different talents, but I also believe that the human mind and body is amazing in its ability to adapt and create an outcome we highly desire. I have experienced what I say is the God effect or divine providence of doing the seemingly impossible! Whatever you need, people, places, things, and abilities would come from out of nowhere to help you achieve as you actively pursue your goals.

The spirit in any human is limitless and it empowers you to do amazing things once you have made a full commitment to a cause. When you can see yourself achieving something, you should speak it as if it were done already, believing it soon will be. For example, saying, "I am strong," even though you're weak, but after the declaration, you go to the gym and stay committed and you will become strong as in your mind you already are. Don't make the mistake many do of just naming and claiming things without extreme effort behind the words. Faith without work is dead. You show your faith by doing the work necessary that will allow your spirit to step in and take your work to a level that you would not be able to on your own.

To be excellent, your vocabulary should always be filled with phrases like "How can I? I can do it, I will do it, I am great, I am creative, I am loving, I am caring, I am giving, I am smart, I am amazing, I am growing, I am rich, I am building, and soon, it will be even as it is, all things are possible, I am beautiful, I am fast, I will act now today, and whatever is positive leads to excellence."

It is written in ancient scriptures that our words are spirit. "Life and death are in the power of the tongue." Knowing this, you must always be mindful of what you say. People with dumpster juice beliefs have POOP JUICE performance and always use their tongue to bring death to their goals and dreams. You will always hear them use phrases like, "I can't, it is too hard, it won't work, no one has ever done it before, it is too cold, too late, impossible, tomorrow, I am dumb, poor, I am not good enough, others are holding me back, it is not my fault," etc. These people are constantly complaining. They are the opposite of optimistic and they are dream killers—not only killing their own dreams, but also anyone else around them.

Those beliefs and attitudes lead to what I like to call POOP JUICE performance. They don't win, they perform terribly, and are content with it because the majority around them do the same thing. Nothing worse than average being praised and accepted as excellent. Earth is filled with billions of POOP JUICE performers and you are surrounded by hundreds. You must protect yourself from them by continually reading and listening to whatever is good, loving, and positive to drown out their negativity and dumpster juice opinions. Hang out with others who know that nothing is impossible and help each other achieve excellence in all you do.

The main reason that billions have POOP JUICE performance is because they don't know who they are. If we all knew who we are, it would be a much better world. So, who are you? It is written that love created the heavens and Earth and all life form by his word. Later, we find that humans are created in the image and likeness of God. Some believe we are gods.

You are a human being, the highest life form on this planet. Humans have dominion over this planet and have the right to create anything they can imagine. Unfortunately, the few that know this have used their power not only to rule the lesser life forms but to enslave and rule other humans as well. Your imagination is a gift from God and you are supposed to use it to create a better world for yourselves. Fear and ignorance keeps most people right where they are. I believe you should feel obligated to help, inform, and open the eyes of your fellow man, and in doing so, you live an excellent existence. We help awaken dreamers, who all have the power to make great contributions to our world in which we all benefit.

You have greatness in you. You should read many books on the subject of humans and their miraculous feats and accomplishments. The more you read, the more you will believe that if they can do it, you can too. You were created to create. You can do it even if no one else has! To be the first is very powerful and many will follow soon after. The great teachings of

Jesus in the bible, Og Mandino, Jeffery Gitomer, Napoleon Hill, Bob Proctor, Myles Munroe, Joe Girard, Zig Ziglar, and many, many others write about the greatness in you. Greater is he that is in you than he that is of the world!

Remember, people take advantage of the ignorant and make them their slaves or footstool. The quote, "My people perish for lack of knowledge," is a reminder to keep learning. You must study to show yourself to be a person who won't be ashamed when called upon to perform. Those who don't study and do mindful practices have POOP JUICE performances because they don't know who they are and what they are capable of, or they are just lazy and unwilling to do the work. So, no matter what area you are interested in, there are books and people you can learn from. But always remember, you have a resource within you that can help you create things that have never been thought of before. If you dream or think it, you can create it. Everything you see was once in someone's mind as an idea before it became physical matter. Everything you see in this physical world was a thought, idea, or dream first in a human mind. No person is gifted with greater gifts than you. We all have unique gifts and talents. If we share them with the world, it will bring us fulfillment.

So, excellence the EZ way is only my personal application of universal principles that will serve you just as they served me. You can go from POOP JUICE to excellent in 90 days or less. Excellence requires focused, mindful attention to the right actions while pursuing your goal. No matter what you do, get an understanding of what you are doing by paying attention and never just doing things in a mindless manner. The mind and body creates muscle memory when you do something over and over. Just make sure it is the right thing and then you will be able to do it without thinking and flow with effortless ease and achieve EZ EXCELLENCE!

www.ingramcontent.com/pod-product-compliance
Lightning Source LLC
LaVergne TN
LVHW021810060526
838201LV00058B/3318